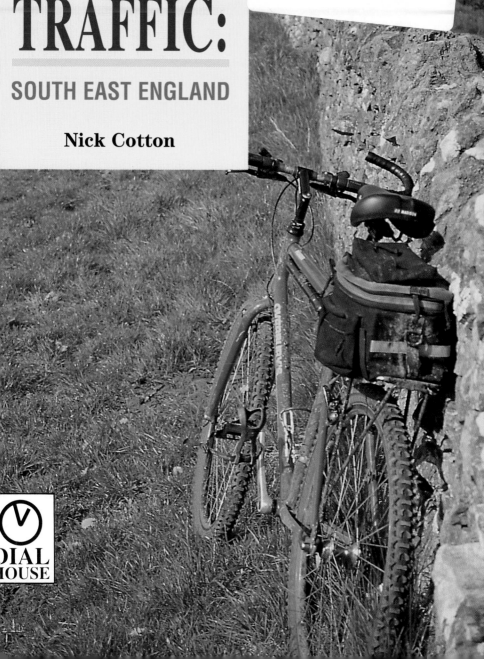

CYCLING
without
TRAFFIC:

SOUTH EAST ENGLAND

Nick Cotton

DIAL
HOUSE

First published 1994
Revised reprint 1998

ISBN 0 7110 2554 1

© Nick Cotton 1994/1998

Published by Dial House
an imprint of Ian Allan Ltd, Terminal House, Station
Approach, Shepperton, Surrey TW17 8AS;

Printed by Ian Allan Printing Ltd, Coombelands House,
Coombelands Lane, Addlestone, Weybridge, Surrey
KT15 1HY.

Publisher's note:
Whilst every effort has been made to ensure the
accuracy of the information contained within this book,
neither Ian Allan Publishing nor the author can accept
any liability arising from the use of the book. In
particular readers will appreciate that only the most
general information regarding open times and
refreshment facilities can be given and intending users
are advised to check prior to their visit.

Previous page: *Nick Cotton*
This page: The open road! *Stockfile*

CONTENTS 🚲

For the last five years, bike sales have outnumbered car sales. More and more people are realising that cycling is good for both health and well-being. However, there is still an increasing number of vehicles on the roads which means that even minor lanes can be busy with traffic and potentially dangerous to ride on, particularly with children in tow.

This book describes 30 easy, waymarked routes where you can cycle away from traffic and gives further information about where else to ride, together with addresses of authorities and organisations which produce cycling leaflets.

Picture: Stockfile

🚲 **KEY MAP**

South East Area

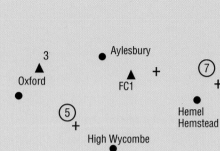

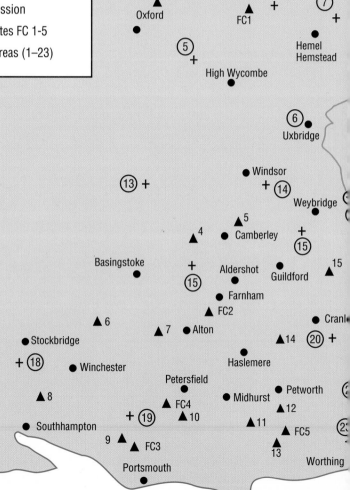

Legend:

- Town/City
- + Routes (1–30)
- ▲ Forestry Commission
  Waymarked routes FC 1-5
  Other forestry areas (1–23)

① +

Bedford + ③

+ ② Milton Keynes

▲ 1 ▲ 2

3 ▲ Oxford ●

● Aylesbury

▲ FC1 + ⑦ +

⑤ + High Wycombe ●

● Hemel Hemstead

⑥ ● Uxbridge

⑬ +

● Windsor

+ ⑭ Weybridge ●

▲ 5

▲ 4 ● Camberley

+ ⑮ 15 ▲

● Basingstoke

+ ⑮ ● Aldershot ● Guildford

● Farnham

▲ FC2

▲ 6 ▲ 7 ● Alton

▲ 14 ⑳ + Cranl

● Stockbridge

+ ⑱ ● Winchester

● Haslemere

● Petersfield

● Petworth

▲ 8

● Midhurst ▲ 12

+ ⑲ ▲ FC4 ▲ 10 ▲ 11 ▲ FC5

● Southhampton

9 ▲ ▲ FC3 ▲ 13 Worthing

● Portsmouth

Braintree
+
④

● Hertford

+
⑩

+ ⑪

● Waltham Abbey
+ ⑫

ONDON

Maidstone ●

⑳⑨
+

▲ 23

● Canterbury

20 ▲ ▲ 21

▲ 22

● Ashford

Dover ●

⑳①   ⑳②
+   +

● Tunbridge
   Wells

East
Grinstead

▲ 19
▲
18

● Tenterden

Hythe ●
+
㉚

⑳⑧

㉔
+

Lewes

nton

㉕
+

⑳⑦
16 ▲ +
     ● Hailsham
▲ 17
+
㉖

● Rye

Eastbourne

Every attempt has been made to bring together all the trails and areas within the Southeast where it is possible to cycle on reasonably flat, good-quality tracks where there are no cars or, in the case of certain country parks, minimal traffic. However, it must be accepted that such a guide can never be fully comprehensive as new developments are continually being implemented as local authorities respond to the demand for the provision of more safe cycle trails.

The trails can be divided into five categories:

1. DISMANTLED RAILWAYS

The vast majority of Britain's railway system was built in the 50 years from 1830 to 1880. After the invention of the car and the development of the road network from the turn of the 20th century onwards, the railways went into decline and in the 1960s many of the lines were closed and the tracks lifted. This was the famous 'Beeching Axe'. It is a great tragedy that Dr Beeching was not a keen leisure cyclist! Had he set in motion the development of leisure cycle trails along the course of the railways he was so busy closing then we could boast one of the finest recreational cycling networks in the world.

As it is, many of the railways were sold off in small sections to adjacent landowners and the continuity of long sections of dismantled track was lost. Thirty years on, some local authorities have risen to the challenge, seized the opportunity and created some fine trails along the course of dismantled railways. The Downs Link, the Cuckoo Trail, routes east and west of East Grinstead and four routes in Hertfordshire are all good examples. Other authorities have done

absolutely nothing and as time goes by the opportunities for creating trails diminish still further as the land is put to other uses. Dismantled railways make good cycle trails for two reasons. First, the gradients tend to be very gentle, and secondly, the broad stone base is ideal for the top dressing which creates a smooth, firm surface for bicycles. Twelve of the 30 rides described in this book are along dismantled railways.

Picture: *Stockfile*

To find out what your own authority intends to do in the future about cycle trails in your area, contact the planning department of your county council (see Useful Addresses page 111). Alternatively, if you wish to get involved on a national level, contact Sustrans, 35 King Street, Bristol BS1 4DZ (Tel: 0117 926 8893), the organisation building the 6,500-mile National Cycle Network which will be completed in the year 2005. The Millennium Routes, covering the first 2,500 miles of the network, will be ready by the year 2000.

2. FORESTRY COMMISSION LAND

There are nine waymarked trails on forestry land:

1/2:	Aston Hill and Wendover
3:	Alice Holt, south of Farnham
4:	North Boarhunt, northwest of Fareham
5:	Queen Elizabeth Park, south of Petersfield
6:	Houghton, northwest of Arundel
7/8:	Friston, west of Eastbourne
9:	Bedgebury, southwest of Cranbrook.

As a general rule, it is permissible to cycle on the hard forestry tracks in other woodland owned by the Forestry Commission, but there are some exceptions. The chapter on the Forestry Commission (see page 106) gives details of the locations of their sites, and addresses and phone numbers of regional offices so that you can find out the exact regulations (which may change at any time due to logging operations).

The area to the south and southwest of London is particularly well-blessed with woodlands appropriate for cycling: there are some 20 large holdings owned by the Forestry Commission with open access to the woodland if you stay on the hard forest roads.

3. CANAL TOWPATHS

The British Waterways Board has undertaken a national survey of its 2000 miles of towpath to see what percentage is suitable for cycling. Unfortunately, the initial results are not very encouraging — only about 10 per cent meet the specified requirements. However, the proportion is much higher in the southeast of the country. In certain cases regional waterways boards have co-ordinated with local authorities and the Countryside Commission to improve the towpaths for all users. It is to be hoped that this collaboration continues and extends throughout the country.

Cycling along canal towpaths can provide plenty of interest — wildlife, barges and locks — and the gradient tends to be flat. However, even the best-quality towpaths are not places to cycle fast as they are often busy with anglers and walkers and it is rare that cycling two abreast is feasible.

The chapter on canals (see page 104) gives you a map of the canal network in the Southeast and details of the waterways boards to contact for further information about the towpaths nearest to you.

4. RESERVOIRS

Large reservoirs can sometimes provide excellent cycling opportunities: the rides are circular, the setting is often very beautiful and there is the added attraction of waterfowl to see. Two rides around reservoirs are described in full: Bewl Water in the heart of Kent and Grafham Water, north of Bedford. Both reservoirs have bike-hire centres.

5. CYCLING ELSEWHERE

If you wish to venture beyond the relatively protected world of cycle trails, there are two choices: write away for leaflets produced by local authorities describing rides on quiet lanes through the countryside (details are given on page 109), or devise your own route.

Should you choose the second course, study the relevant Ordnance Survey Landranger map: the yellow roads represent the smaller, quieter lanes. When cycling off-road, you must stay on legal rights of way. It is illegal to cycle on footpaths, but you are allowed to use bridleways, byways open to all traffic (BOATs) and roads used as public paths (RUPPs). These are all marked on Ordnance Survey maps. Devising routes 'blind' can sometimes be a bit of a hit-or-miss affair, however. Some tracks may turn out to be very muddy and overgrown, and other hazards include blocked paths, locked gates and inadequate or non-existent waymarking. If you feel strongly about the condition of a right of way, contact the rights of way department of your local authority and tell them about the problems you have found.

Facing Picture: *Nick Cotton*

THE COUNTRY CODE

- Enjoy the countryside and respect its life and work.
- Guard against all risk of fire.
- Fasten all gates.
- Keep your dogs under close control.
- Keep to rights of way across farmland.
- Use gates and stiles to cross fences, hedges and walls.
- Leave livestock, crops and machinery alone.
- Take your litter home.
- Help to keep all water clean.
- Protect wildlife, plants and trees.
- Take special care on country roads.
- Make no unnecessary noise.

NO THROUGH ROAD FOR MOTOR VEHICLES

Bicycles should be thoroughly overhauled on a regular basis but there are certain things worth checking before each ride, and knowledge of how to mend a puncture is essential.

The four most important things to check are:

1. Do both the front and rear brakes work effectively?
2. Are the tyres inflated hard?
3. Is the chain oiled?
4. Is the saddle the right height? (Low enough when sitting in the saddle to be able to touch the ground with your toes, high enough to have your leg almost straight when you are pedalling.)

Other clickings, grindings, gratings, crunchings, rattlings, squeakings, wobblings and rubbings either mean that your bike needs oiling and parts need adjusting, or a trip to your local bike mechanic is long overdue. Try to give a bike shop as much warning as possible; do not expect to turn up and have your bike fixed on the spot.

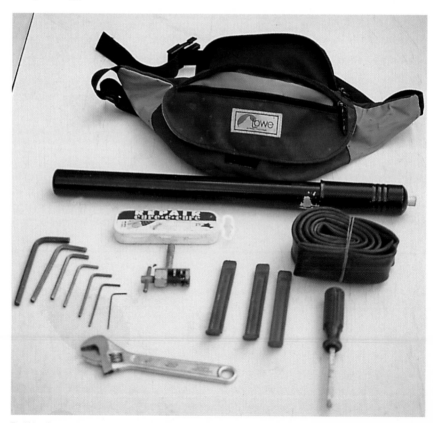

Tool kit - the essentials: pump, repair kit, spare inner tube, allen keys, spanner, screwdriver, chain link remover, tyre lever. *Nick Cotton*

MENDING A PUNCTURE

You will need:

- a spanner to undo the nuts holding the wheel to the frame
- tyre levers to ease the tyre off the rim
- glue and patches
- a pump

These items should always be carried, even on short rides, as walking with a bike with a flat tyre is not much fun.

1. Remove the wheel which has the puncture, using a spanner to undo the nuts on the hub if it is not fitted with quick-release levers. (You will probably have to unhitch the brake cable in order to remove the wheel.)

2. Remove the tyre from the rim, using tyre levers if the fit is tight. Insert two levers under the rim a few inches apart and push on them together to free the tyre from the rim, taking care not to pinch the inner tube. Work the levers around the rim until the tyre is completely free.

3. Remove the dust cap and any locking ring from the valve. Push the valve inside the tyre then gently pull the inner tube out.

4. Partially inflate the tyre and pass it close to your ear until you hear a hiss (or close to your cheek or lips to feel the escaping air). Locate the puncture and mark it with a cross, using the crayon you should have in the puncture repair kit. (It is not often that you need to use a bucket of water to locate a puncture: you can almost always hear it or feel it.)

5. Deflate the tyre, by pushing in the valve. Hold the tyre so that the section with the puncture is tight over your knuckles. If you have sandpaper in the repair kit, lightly roughen the area around the puncture.

6. Spread glue thinly over the puncture, covering an area slightly larger than the patch you are going to use. Leave to dry for at least five minutes. This is the stage at which many people go wrong: they try to fix the patch too soon. The glue is not an adhesive, it is actually melting the rubber.

7. While waiting for the glue to do its stuff, check the inside of the tyre for any obvious thorn or piece of glass which may have caused the puncture. Run your finger slowly and sensitively around the inside of the tyre to see if you can find the cause of the puncture.

8. After waiting at least five minutes for the glue, select a patch, remove the foil and push the patch firmly into the middle of the gluey area. Peel off the backing paper. If you have a lump of chalk in the repair kit, dust the area with some grated chalk.

9. Replace the tube inside the tyre, starting by pushing the valve through the hole in the rim. Ensure that the tube is completely inside the tyre then using only your hands (ie NOT the tyre levers), gently ease the tyre back inside the rim. The last section will be the hardest, use the heel of the palms of your hands and your thumbs to roll the last part back inside the rim.

10. Re-inflate the tyre, replace the locking ring and the dust cap. Replace the wheel into the frame of the bike and do the nuts up tightly, ensuring that it is set centrally (check by spinning the wheel and seeing if it rubs against the frame). Re-attach the brakes if you have detached the cable.

BICYCLE HIRE

Some of the more popular cycling areas now have bike-hire centres, notably at the large reservoirs and some of the designated Forestry Commission trails. They offer a good opportunity to test different bikes, to give a non-cyclist a chance of trying out cycling, or can save the hassle of loading up and carrying your own bikes to the start of a trail. Wherever cycle-hire centres exist, they are mentioned in the route descriptions in the Essential Information section. It is a good idea to ring beforehand and book a bike, particularly on summer weekends and during the school holidays.

No matter what you do, you'll always get a puncture at some time! Be prepared. *Stockfile*

Comfort, freedom of movement and protection against the unexpected shower should be the three guiding factors in deciding what to wear when you go cycling. Specialist cycling clothing is by no means essential to enjoyable cycling, particularly on the short and easy rides contained in this book.

Starting from the top:

HELMET AND HEADGEAR

The issue of wearing helmets often provokes controversy. Let us hope that it forever remains a matter of personal choice. A helmet does not prevent accidents from happening. Nevertheless, most serious injuries to cyclists are head injuries and helmets can reduce impact.

The case for children wearing helmets is much stronger: they are far more likely to cause damage to themselves by losing control and falling over than an adult. It may be difficult at first to avoid the strap 'pinching' when putting a helmet on a child's head. Bribery of some form or other, once the helmet is securely in place, often helps to persuade the child to see the helmet as a good thing.

In cold weather, a woolly hat or a balaclava is the most effective way of keeping warm. Twenty per cent of body heat is lost through the head.

THE UPPER BODY

It is better to have several thin layers of clothing rather than one thick sweater or coat so that you can make fine adjustments to achieve the most comfortable temperature. Zips or buttons on sleeves and the front of garments also allow you to adjust the temperature.

Try putting your arms right out in front of you — is the clothing tight over your

back? If so, you should wear something a bit looser.

If you are intending to cycle regularly when it is cold, it is worth investing in good-quality thermal underwear and synthetic fleece jackets. These help perspiration to dissipate, do not hold water and dry quickly.

A small woollen scarf and gloves (together with the woolly hat mentioned above) take up very little space and enable you to cope with quite a drop in temperature.

WATERPROOFS

You are far more at risk from exposure on a wet and windy day than a cold, dry day. The biggest danger lies in getting thoroughly soaked when a strong wind is blowing. Unless you are absolutely certain that it will not rain, it is always worth packing something waterproof. A light, showerproof cagoule takes up little space. If you are buying a waterproof top specifically for cycling, buy a very bright coloured jacket with reflective strips so that you are visible when light is poor.

LEGS

As with the upper body, what you should be looking for is something comfortable which does not restrict your movement. Tight, non-stretch trousers would be the worst thing to wear — uncomfortable at the knees and the hips and full of thick seams that dig in! Baggy track suit bottoms tend to get caught in the chain and can hold a lot of water if it rains. The best things to wear are leggings or tracksters that are fairly tight at the ankle. However, if you feel reluctant about looking like a ballet dancer, then a long pair of socks worn over the bottom of your trousers keeps them from getting oily or caught in the chain.

Stockfile

CYCLING SHORTS

If you are going to do a lot of cycling then cycling shorts should be the first piece of specialist clothing you buy. They give a lot of padding while allowing your legs to move freely.

FOOTWEAR

Almost any shoe with a reasonably flat sole is appropriate, although you should bear in mind that few of the trails are sealed with tarmac so there may well be puddles or even mud in some cases after rain. A pair of trainers or old tennis shoes are a good bet.

NB. Take care to ensure that shoe laces are tied and are not dangling where they could get caught in the chain. The same goes for straps on backpacks and straps on panniers, or particularly long scarves!

WHAT TO TAKE

- Hat, scarf, gloves
- Waterproof
- Drink (water or squash is better than fizzy drinks)
- Snacks (fruit, dried fruit, nuts, malt loaf, oatbars)
- Tool kit (pump, puncture repair kit, small adjustable spanner, reversible screwdriver, set of allen keys, tyre levers, chain link extractor)
- Guide book and map (map holder)
- Money
- Camera
- Lock
- Lights and reflective belt (if there is the remotest possibility of being out after dusk)

You can either carry the above in a day-pack on your back or in panniers that fit on to a rack at the rear of the bike. Panniers are the best bet as they do not restrict your movement and do not make your back sweaty.

Facing Picture: *Nick Cotton*

In theory there are three ways of getting to the start of a ride: cycling there from home; catching a train and cycling to your start point, or carrying the bikes on a car.

If you drive, there are three ways of transporting the bikes:

INSIDE THE CAR

With quick-release skewers now fitted on many new bikes (on the saddle and wheels), it is usually easy to take bikes apart quickly and to fit them into the back of most hatchback cars. If you are carrying more than one bike inside the car you should put an old blanket between each bike to protect paintwork and delicate gear mechanisms from damage.

If you would like to carry your bike(s) inside your car and the idea of quick-release skewers appeals to you, these can normally be fitted by your local bike shop.

Bear in mind that the bikes may be wet and/or muddy when you get back to the car so carry sheets or blankets to protect the upholstery of your car.

ON TOP OF THE CAR

You can buy special roof-racks which fit on top of cars to carry bikes. On some the bikes are carried upside down, others the right way up; on others the right way up with the front wheel removed.

The advantages of this system are that the bikes are kept separate one from the other (ie they do not rub against each other), you can get things out of the boot without problem and they do not obscure visibility.

The disadvantages of this system are that you need to be reasonably tall and strong to lift the bikes up on to the roof, it adds considerably to fuel consumption and feels somewhat precarious in strong crosswinds.

ON THE BACK OF THE CAR

This system seems to be the most versatile and popular method. Different racks can fit almost any sort of car with the use of clips, straps and adjustable angles.

The advantages of this system are that the rack itself folds down to a small space, the rack can be used on a variety of different cars, you do not need to be particularly tall or strong to load bikes on to the rack and fuel consumption is not as badly affected as by bikes on the top.

The disadvantages of this system are that you may well need to buy a separate, hang-on number plate and rear lighting system if the number plate, braking

Stockfile

Tie all straps with proper knots. Bows are not good enough.

Use stretch rubber bungees for extra security, particularly to ensure that the bottom of the bikes is attached to the bumper if you are carrying the bikes on the back of the car.

If the number plate or brake lights and indicators are obscured you are legally obliged to hang a separate number plate and lights from the back of the bikes.

It is essential to check and double check all the fixings before setting off and to stop and check again during the course of the journey to ensure nothing has slipped or come loose.

If you are leaving the bikes on the car for any length of time, lock the bikes to each other and to the rack. While on your ride, it is as well to remove the rack and to lock it inside your car.

lights and indicators are obscured by the bikes; the bikes are pressed one against the other and may rub off paintwork; you will restrict access to the boot/hatchback.

The deluxe system fits on to the back of a towbar, has its own lighting system and keeps the bikes separate as they fit into individual grooved rails. You can buy systems which hold two, three or four bikes.

GENERAL RULES ABOUT CARRYING BIKES

Remove all pumps, lights, panniers, water bottles and locks from the bikes before loading them on to the rack.

Lengths of pipe insulation material are useful for protecting the bikes from rubbing against each other. Try to avoid having delicate parts such as gear mechanisms pushed up against the frame or spokes of the adjoining bike.

BIKES ON TRAINS

The regulations for carrying bikes on trains seem to change each year and vary from one operator to another, one sort of train to another and according to different times of the day and different days of the week. The only advice that can possibly be given that will remain useful is to take nothing for granted and ALWAYS phone before turning up at the station to find out charges and availability of bike space. Even then you may find that incorrect information is given out: it is always best to go to the station and talk in person to station staff.

Since privatisation different companies have adopted different approaches to carrying bikes on trains. The first step is to call the central number 0345 484950 and ask them if there are any restrictions on bikes on the train which you want to catch ie how many bikes are allowed on the train, is there a charge, does the space need to be booked in advance?

AROUND GRAFHAM WATER

(10 miles north of Bedford)

Grafham Water is similar to Rutland Water, which lies 30 miles to the northwest (covered in the *Midlands and Peak District* book in the 'Cycling Without Traffic' series). This reservoir provides an excellent circular cycling route around the perimeter of the water. There are refreshment stops in or near Perry village, an Exhibition Centre at Marlow Park and cycle-hire facilities. Indeed, this is one of the best routes in the region to try out cycling again if it is some years since you were last on a bike.

Background and Places of Interest

Grafham Water
This is a man-made reservoir. It was constructed in 1966 by flooding a shallow valley and is the third largest lake of this kind in England, holding 59,000 million litres of water. It is an important nesting site for many species of birds.

Exhibition Centre at Marlow car park
Open 11.00am-4.00pm Monday to Friday and 11.00am-5.00pm Saturday and Sunday.

Huntingdon
Fine Georgian houses form the heart of this handsome old town. Renowned as the birthplace of Oliver Cromwell in 1599, it has museums of Cromwellian relics in the former grammar school. A 14th-century bridge leads over the Great Ouse to the twin town of Godmanchester, a treasure-house of varied architectural styles.

Wood Green Animal Shelter
(1 mile south of Godmanchester on the A1198) Animals ranging from hamsters to horses can be seen here. Open daily all year 9.00am-3.00pm. Tel: 01480 830014.

St Neots
A compact, ancient market town with interesting old inns, narrow streets and a fine market square.

Starting Point: Grafham Water is just off the A1 between St Neots and Huntingdon.

Parking: There are three main car parks around the lake - Mander Park, Plummer Park and Marlow Park. All three are on the circular route around the lake, so you can start at any of them. The only point to bear in mind on a windy day is that it is best to cycle into the wind when you are fresh and do the second half with the wind behind you. The Water Authority suggests doing the ride anti-clockwise to avoid having to cross the road in Perry.

Distance: 10 miles.

Map: Ordnance Survey Landranger Sheet 153.

Hills: Some gentle climbs, but no serious hills.

Surface: Good-quality gravel tracks.

Roads and road crossings: One short road section through Perry village along the south side of the lake.

Refreshments: Cafes in Mander and Marlow Parks; Wheatsheaf pub in Perry village; Montagu Arms, just off the route in Grafham village.

Cycle Hire: Grafham Water Cycling,

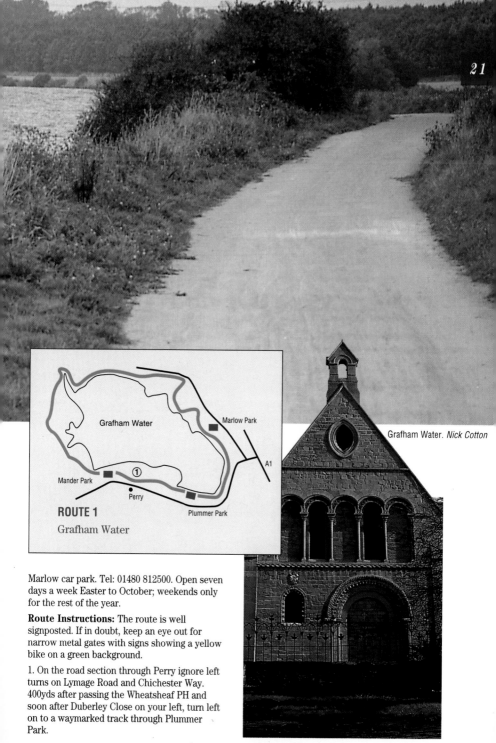

Grafham Water. *Nick Cotton*

ROUTE 1

Grafham Water

Oliver Cromwell Museum in nearby Huntingdon.
AA Picture Library

Marlow car park. Tel: 01480 812500. Open seven days a week Easter to October; weekends only for the rest of the year.

Route Instructions: The route is well signposted. If in doubt, keep an eye out for narrow metal gates with signs showing a yellow bike on a green background.

1. On the road section through Perry ignore left turns on Lymage Road and Chichester Way. 400yds after passing the Wheatsheaf PH and soon after Duberley Close on your left, turn left on to a waymarked track through Plummer Park.

THE MILTON KEYNES REDWAY

There are three routes through Milton Keynes starting from Willen Lakes.

Milton Keynes Redway, a comprehensive network of traffic-free trails, is a leisure cyclist's dream come true, particularly if you are a parent with young children learning to ride. Mile after mile of excellent, broad, tree-lined tracks carefully designed to avoid cars, traffic lights, roundabouts and all the other nightmares of cycling in urban areas. Whatever your preconceptions about Milton Keynes (and I was as guilty of prejudice as the next person when I first arrived), you soon realise that the place was designed to be enjoyed by bike. Send for a copy of the excellent Redway map before turning up (address below). Although it may appear unlikely that some of the best cycling in this book should be in the middle of a new town, try it and see for yourself! *NB. See Waterway Code for Cyclists on page 104.*

Background and Places of Interest

- **Willen Lakes**
The peaceful north lake with its wildfowl, Peace Pagoda, temple, labyrinth and old village contrasts with the busy lively south lake which is the main water-sports area within Milton Keynes.

- **Linford Manor Park**
Attractive landscaped parkland associated with the magnificent 17th-century manor house, buildings and church of the Linford Estate. The almshouses and thatched barn are now an arts centre called The Courtyard.

- **Grand Union Canal**
Built between 1793 and 1805, it became a vital link between London and the industrial Midlands. It was the M1 of its time, providing a direct connection long before the steam train or the lorry. A vast range of goods, from bricks to barley, was carried in the horse-drawn narrowboats. The route became increasingly busy and profitable and then, like all other waterways, the Grand Union Canal suffered overwhelming competition from the new railways at the turn of the 19th century and from the improved road network at the beginning of the 20th century.

- **Woburn Safari Park**
(6 miles southeast of Milton Keynes)
Giraffes, lions and elephants in Britain's largest drive-through safari park. Open daily April to October. Tel: 01525 290407.

Redway cycle path, Milton Keynes. *Stockfile*

ROUTE 2
Milton Keynes

Bridge 76
Black Horse PH
⑦
M1
Grand Union Canal
⑥
V10
North Lake
A509 (H5)
START
⑤
Willen Lake
Bridge 81B
④
canal broadwalk
①
Campbell Park
②
③
Woughton on the Green

Woburn Abbey and Safari Park. *AA Picture Library*

Starting Point: The car park by Willen Lake just off Junction 14 of the M1.

Parking: As above.

Distance:
a. A 2.5-mile circuit around the lakes.
b. The southern route, a 4.5-mile circuit.
c. The northern route, 3.5 miles from the lakes to the Black Horse PH at Great Linford (ie 7 miles round trip).

Map: Ordnance Survey Landranger Sheet 152.

The best map for cycling around Milton Keynes is the Redway Map, showing the vast network of excellent cycle lanes in the area. It costs £1.00 and is available by sending an SAE to: Milton Keynes Tourist Information Centre, The Food Centre, 411 Secklow Gate East, Central Milton Keynes, MK9 3NE. Tel: 01908 232525.

Hills: No serious hills.

Surface: Excellent surface throughout on the Redway. The canal towpath is slightly rougher between bridge 78 (Gifford Park PH) and bridge 76 (Black Horse PH).

Roads and road crossings: None,

Refreshments: Wayfarer PH at the Sports Centre on Willen Lake (South). Gifford Park PH at bridge 78 on the canal towpath. Black Horse PH at bridge 76.

Route Instructions
(a) Anti-clockwise circuit of both Willen Lakes
Follow the redbrick path south towards Woolstone and Kingston, keeping the water on your left and passing the Watersports Centre. Follow waterside track around lakes, aiming towards Willen Village church then the Peace Pagoda then the bandstand near to the start.

(b) Southern Route to Woughton on the Green
1. Follow the start of circuit of lakes described above. After the Watersports Centre, near to miniature railway, ignore first right signposted

'Milton Keynes Village, Ouzel Valley'. Bear left to stay close to the lake then shortly, at T-junction take the next right (same names on signpost) to pass beneath road bridge.

2. Follow the River Ouzel for two miles, crossing three narrow cattle grids and passing a wooden bridge over the river. Soon after passing beneath second road bridge, just before a second wooden river bridge turn sharp right passing fenced-off clumps of trees towards the Canal Broadwalk.

3. Follow signs for Canal Broadwalk. Just before red-brick bridge over the canal, turn right signposted 'Woolstone, Newlands, Campbell Park'.

4. Follow the Canal Broadwalk beneath several bridges. At bridge 81B, a wide bridge with red-brick pillars and a central span of concrete and black railings, turn right signposted 'Peace Pagoda, Willen Lake' to return to the start or continue straight ahead and join the Northern

Route at Instruction 6.

c) Northern Route

5. To get to the Grand Union Canal from the Willen Lakes car park follow signs for 'Newlands/Grand Union Canal/Campbell Park'. Join the canal at bridge 81B. Turn right along the Canal Broadwalk.

6. At bridge 79 cross to the other side and turn right. At the T-junction with Cottisford Crescent (near Marsh Drive/High Street) turn right then second left signposted 'Linford Manor'. At the almshouses turn right and follow this good path past a stone circle as far as the Black Horse PH at Bridge 76.

7. Retrace steps, cross back to the other (east) side of the canal at bridge 78 then leave the canal at bridge 81B (a wide bridge with red-brick pillars and a central concrete span with black railings) signposted 'Willen Lake, Peace Pagoda' to return to the start.

PRIORY COUNTRY PARK
(A ride along the railway path to Willington)

This is a tranquil countryside area close to Bedford town centre. The park, with lakes surrounded by trees and grassland, is a great place to see wildlife. For a longer ride, take the Bedford to Willington Countryway from the entrance to the park on a trail across fields and through woodland along the course of an old railway line.

Background and Places of Interest

• Priory Country Park
This is named after the Augustinian priory established here in the 12th century. Very little of this now remains, although the stone wall between the marina and the sailing lake formed part of the boundary.

• The Visitor Centre
Run by Bedfordshire and Cambridgeshire Wildlife Trust, this houses various exhibitions. Open every day except Saturday.

• The River Ouse
Near to Priory Country Park, at Cardington Lock, the river splits into two, the left waterway passing through the lock to the navigable part of the river. The lock was restored to full working order in the late 1970s, making it possible to cruise from Bedford to the Wash.

• The Royal Society for the Protection of Birds Nature Reserve, The Lodge, Sandy
(east of Sandy on the A422)
A nature reserve in 104 acres of woodland, with walks and nature trails, observation hides, a picnic area and an RSPB shop. Open daily all year 9.00am-5.00pm. Tel: 01767 680551.

The Shuttleworth Collection, Old Warden
(8 miles southeast of Bedford)
A small grass aerodrome, with seven hangars housing some 40 aeroplanes, evoking the early years of aviation. Open daily all year. Tel: 01767 627288.

Nearby is The Swiss Garden, an award-winning, picturesque garden with rare plants, shrubberies and a grotto. Open afternoons (except Tuesdays) March to September. Tel: 01767 627666.

Woburn Safari Park and Leisure Park
(signed from Junction 12/M1)
Britain's largest drive-through safari park. Open daily April to October. Tel: 0525 290407. Also Woburn Abbey and Park, home of the Dukes of Bedford, set in a 3,000-acre deer park. Tel: 01525 290666.

The Shuttleworth Collection, Old Warden.
AA Picture Library

Starting Point: Priory Country Park, signposted off the A428 Bedford/Cambridge road.

Parking: As above.

Distance: 1.5 miles around the lake. 4 miles along the Bedford-Willington Countryway (8-mile round trip).

Map: Ordnance Survey Landranger Sheet 153.

Hills: None.

Surface: There is a short grassy section

on the southern side of the lake.

Roads and road crossings: If you wish to visit The Crown PH and the dovecote in Willington, there is a short section on a very quiet road in the village.

Refreshments: The Priory Marina PH at the start. The Crown PH at Willington.

Route Instructions:
1. The railway path starts close to the car park entrance signposted 'Countryway'.
2. Go past water treatment works. At T-junction with track soon after crossing bridge over the bypass bear left. At T-junction after gravel pits turn right then left (bike signs).

3. At T-junction with narrow tarmac path with a fence ahead turn left, follow the river then turn right opposite bridge. The track ends near to a lake at the Willington-Great Barford road. Retrace steps. (On your return, to visit Willington, turn left at the end of high green wire/concrete post fence. At the road go straight ahead for pub or turn right for 0.75 mile for dovecote).

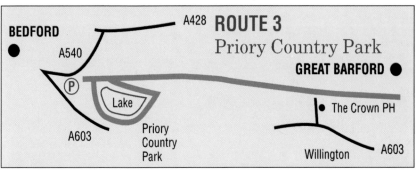

ROUTE 3
Priory Country Park

Stagsden bird gardens. *AA Picture Library*

ROUTE 4 THE FLITCH WAY
(Braintree to Little Dunmow)

The best of Essex's dismantled railways, with the option of a good pub at the end. The Flitch Way follows the line of the old Bishop's Stortford, Dunmow & Braintree Railway, built in the 1860s.

Nearby are the remains of earthworks and castles at Stebbing and Castle Hedingham. Although the Flitch Way runs for 16 miles between Braintree and Bishop's Stortford, it is not open to cyclists along the whole length. The best surface is to be found on the eastern section between Braintree and Great Dunmow.

Background and Places of Interest

• Braintree
A lively market town whose riches derive from trade in wool and textiles, the story of which is told in the Town Hall's Heritage Centre. There are ancient houses in every street and a striking courtyard in the medieval Swan Hotel. The Working Silk Museum, New Mills, South Street, produces silk on the original handlooms. Tel: 0376 553393.

• Colne Valley Railway
(10 miles north of Braintree)
Vintage steam trains take passengers along a lovingly restored section of the old Colne Valley and Halstead Railway. Near by is Castle Hedingham, a village dominated by a vast Norman keep built in 1140 with a well-preserved banqueting hall and minstrels' gallery.

Starting Point and Parking: Braintree railway station. The Flitch Way starts at the end of the car park furthest away from the trains.

Distance: 6.5 miles (13 miles round trip).

Map: Ordnance Survey Sheet 167.

Hills: None.

Surface: Good, broad, stone-based track on the length described.

Roads and road crossings:
(1) There is an alternative to the crossing of the fast and busy A120 which involves a short section on a quiet road — see instructions below.

(2) A short section on a quiet lane connects the Flitch Way with the pub in Little Dunmow.

(3) If you wish to continue into Great Dunmow, there is the fast A120 to cross followed by a mile along a fairly busy road into the town centre.

Refreshments: Flitch of Bacon PH at Little Dunmow.

Route Instructions:
1. Follow the Flitch Way westwards from Braintree railway station car park. After 2.5 miles, at the far end of the old station and platform at Rayne, turn left off the railway path via a white wooden gate on to School Road then bear right. Cross the bridge over the A120 then take the second No Through Road to the right (Mill Road). After 1 mile, just before the bridge over the railway, turn right downhill by a Flitch Way signpost. Descend to the railway path and turn left. Remember this point for the return trip.

2. After 3.5 miles the trail descends to the Felsted-Little Dunmow road. Turn right then sharply left, then opposite a red-brick house bear right to rejoin the track. Immediately after passing beneath the next red-brick bridge turn right off the railway path and join a minor lane (remember this point for the return). Turn left on the lane then at the T-junction at the end of Brook Street, turn left again for the Flitch of Bacon PH.

3. (From Little Dunmow to Braintree) With your back to the Flitch of Bacon PH turn right then take the second No Through Road to the right (Brook Road). Just after the playing fields to the right, turn right by a Flitch Way signpost to descend to the railway path. Turn left. At the road turn right then left to climb back up on to the course of the railway path.

4. Easily missed! (This detour is to avoid a dangerous crossing of the busy A120.) After 3.5 miles, immediately after the third red-brick bridge turn right off the railway path uphill to a minor lane. Turn left on the lane for 1 mile. At the T-junction with a wider road turn left, cross the bridge over the A120 then as the road swings right rejoin the railway path by the old station at Rayne and turn right for Braintree.

Facing Picture: Colne Valley Railway. *AA Picture Library*

Great Dunmow

A120

Little Dunmow
Flitch of Bacon PH

②

①
Rayne

BRAINTREE

③ Felsted

④
very busy
road crossing

Alternative
route on
quiet lanes,
with safe
crossing

Ⓟ
railway station
START

ROUTE 4

The Flitch Way,
Braintree

Nick Cotton

THE RIDGEWAY AND ICKNIELD WAY

(Watlington, west of High Wycombe)

This 10-mile stretch of the Ridgeway represents one of its flattest and best-maintained sections.

It crosses a mixture of woodland and open arable country. It is not a trail in the same sense as a dismantled railway or towpath and the quality of the surface may change to quite some degree in the winter or after prolonged rain which will make going slower and muddier.

The Ridgeway is one of the oldest highways in Europe, and possibly the world.

Background and Places of Interest

• The Ridgeway
The 85-mile long trail is based on two very ancient highways, the Wessex upland way known as the Ridgeway, which goes down to the Thames at Streatley, and the Icknield Way, which continues the line northeast from Goring on the east bank of the Thames.

These 85 miles represent only the middle section of a much longer route that stretched as far southwest as the Dorset coast via Stonehenge and the Salisbury Plain, and as far northeast as the Norfolk coast via the flint mines of Grime's Graves.

Prehistoric man preferred the chalk uplands where the going was drier underfoot and less impeded by vegetation than the thick forest that would have covered the plains and lowlands.

• Aston Rowant Nature Reserve
(3 miles northeast of Watlington)
Chalk downland, scrub and beechwoods on Beacon Hill, with views across the Vale of Aylesbury. Look out for fox, badger and deer.

• Ewelme
(3 miles southwest of Watlington)
One of the most picturesque of the Chiltern villages, with a group of 15th-century buildings.

• Wallingford
A market town and riverside resort. It is a strategic crossing point of the Thames, with towpath walks and fine Georgian houses. A steam railway runs 1.25 miles south from Wallingford to the village of Cholsey.

Facing Picture: The Ridgeway has some demanding hills - Coombe Hill near Wendover. *Stockfile*

Starting Point: The free car park in Watlington (southwest of M40 Jct 6), signposted from the centre of the town.

Parking: As above. Or you may wish to park on the Ridgeway itself, 0.5 mile southeast of Chinnor on the road towards Bledlow Ridge.

Distance: 3 miles southwest along the Ridgeway (6 miles round trip). 7.5 miles northeast along the Ridgeway to the pub at Bledlow (15 miles round trip).

Maps: Ordnance Survey Landranger Sheets 165 and 175.

Hills: A short, gentle climb on tarmac to the start. The Ridgeway itself is gently undulating, hovering around the 150 metre contour on this section of its course.

There is a drop of 130ft into Bledlow, hence a climb of 130ft on your return.

Surface: Varies from excellent stone-based track to hard-packed earth with some roots showing through. You are likely to come across puddles and mud after heavy rain and from mid-autumn to late spring.

Roads and road crossings: Both routes start and end with 0.5 mile on a quiet road between the car park and the start of the Ridgeway. One fairly busy road (the B480) must be crossed if you are heading southwest. One major road (the A40) to cross heading northeast. The latter is not as busy as you might expect as almost all the traffic goes on the parallel M40.

Refreshments:
Some choice in Watlington.
No refreshments *en route* on the southwest section, although the woods at the end look good for a picnic. The Lions of Bledlow PH lies at the end of the northeast section. There are also pubs in Chinnor and along the B4009, although this road is not recommended for cycling as it can be quite busy.

Route Instructions :
(Southwest)
1. Leave the car park and turn right, following one-way signs. Go past the Carriers Arms PH and up the gentle hill. 300yds past the hospital, and before the hill becomes very steep, at a crossroads of gravel tracks, turn right.

2. Take care at the crossroads with the B480. Go straight ahead, signposted 'Lys Mill/Dame Alice Farm'. After 400yds, as the tarmac swings sharply right, carry on straight ahead on to a gravel track, following signs for the Ridgeway and Icknield Way.

3. The surface becomes a bit bumpy through

the woodland, but improves once out of the trees. Cross a second (quiet) road. You will pass Britwell House on your right and away in the distance you should see the distinctive shapes of the cooling towers of Didcot power station.

4. It is suggested that you go only as far as the road at the edge of the beechwood on your left then return to the start. Beyond this point the bridleway/cycling route, now called Swan's Way, follows quiet lanes southwest into Goring where it crosses the Thames. Running parallel to Swan's Way for this section, the Ridgeway has footpath status and is not open to cyclists. The two trails meet in Goring.

(Northeast)
A. Follow route direction 1 above to the crossroads of gravel tracks. Turn left.

Wallingford bridge and church. *AA Picture Library*

ROUTE 5

The Ridgeway from Watlington

The track soon becomes rutted, although it is being improved.

B. Go underneath the M40, then at the crossroads with the A40 go straight ahead on to the continuation of the Ridgeway and the Icknield Way.

C. After 3.5 miles, having crossed two more roads and passed a factory on the left, you will come to a large red-brick house where the Ridgeway swings sharply right. At this point you could either return (the Ridgeway soon starts climbing steeply) or carry on straight ahead downhill on the track (signposted 'Swans Way') to the pub in Bledlow.

D. At a T-junction with another track, turn left for 200yds to reach the Lions of Bledlow PH. (Remember this junction for your return trip.)

THE GRAND UNION CANAL
*(Between Paddington and Marsworth
near Tring)*

Towpaths along rivers and canals are the best escape routes from the centre of London. The Thames towpath leads on via the Wey Navigation to the Basingstoke Canal. The Lee and Stort Navigation exits London to the north towards Waltham Abbey and Hertford. This ride uses the Grand Union Canal which heads west as far as West Drayton before cutting north towards Uxbridge, where the canal surroundings take on a much greener aspect, and then continues on to Rickmansworth and Berkhamsted. It has many points in its favour: the surface is generally very good, there are several convenient starting points with car parking and the train runs parallel to the canal for much of its length, enabling you to take the train out and cycle back, or vice versa. There are many refreshment stops along the way and much of interest by way of boating activity and birdlife.
NB. See the Waterway Code for Cyclists on page 105.

Picture: *Stockfile*

Background and Places of Interest

• The Grand Union Canal
This is unique among English canals, being composed of at least eight separate canals. The system links London with Birmingham, Leicester and Nottingham. Up to the 1920s all these canals were owned by quite separate companies. In 1929 the whole system was integrated as the Grand Union Canal.

The original part of the system was the Grand Junction Canal, built at the turn of the 18th century to provide a short cut from Braunston, on the Oxford Canal, to Brentford, on the Thames. It cut a full 60 miles off the previous route via Oxford and, with its 14ft-wide locks and numerous branches to important towns, rapidly became busy and profitable.

The building of wide locks to take 70-ton barges was a brave attempt to persuade neighbouring canal companies to widen their navigations and establish a 70-ton barge standard throughout the waterways of the Midlands. Unfortunately, the other companies were deterred by the cost of widening and to this day can only accommodate boats 7ft wide. The history of the English canals might have been very different had the Grand Junction's attempt succeeded.

These canals made up the spine of southern England's transport system until the advent of the railways, playing an essential role in the Industrial Revolution. All kinds of goods, ranging from bricks to barley, were carried in horse-drawn narrowboats.

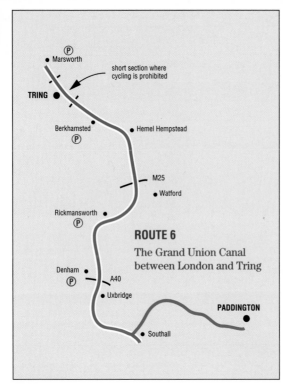

Marsworth P

short section where
cycling is prohibited

TRING

Berkhamsted P

Hemel Hempstead

M25

Watford

Rickmansworth P

ROUTE 6

The Grand Union Canal
between London and Tring

Denham P

A40

Uxbridge

PADDINGTON

Southall

Starting Points:

1. Marsworth (near Tring) 6 miles east of
Aylesbury at the car park off the B489 by the
bridge over the Grand Union Canal next to the
White Lion PH. (NB. If you are heading south
from Marsworth, there is a short section
between bridges 133 and 137 where cycling on
the towpath is prohibited and you will have to
use road alternatives.)

2. Berkhamsted. Free car park at the end of the
main street heading towards Tring, opposite the
Lamb PH down St John's Well Lane.

3. Hemel Hempstead. From the Magic
Roundabout at the junction of the A414 with the
A4146, exit on to Lawn Lane signposted
'Bennetts End, Nash Mills'. At the traffic lights
turn right down Durrants Hill Road then right
again just after the Albion PH and the bridge.

4. Rickmansworth Aquadrome. (This is
complicated, as you have to do a full circuit of a
roundabout.) Follow signs for the A404, London
and Northwood out of Rickmansworth. At the
Moor Lane roundabout shortly after the White
Bear PH, where Watford (A415) is signposted
straight ahead and London (A404)off to the

right, do a circuit of the
roundabout to head back towards
the town centre then turn first left
on to Harefield Road. Take the
first right after Tesco supermarket
on to a No Through Road,
Frogmoor Lane, signposted
Aquadrome.

5. Denham Park. Take the A40
exit from Junction 1 of the M40
then take the first right. Follow
signs for Denham Park and Colne
Valley Park. Park in the furthest
car park on the right. From the far
end of the car park follow the
bridleway leading away from the
car park into the wood. Cross the
wooden bridge then shortly after
passing the wire fence of the golf
course on your left, take the next
stone track right to join the
towpath at bridge 182.

Parking: As above.

British Rail: This is an excellent
ride for making use of the train, as
there are many stations close to
the canal allowing you to catch
the train in one direction then
cycle back to your starting point.
Stations to consider are Tring,
Berkhamsted, Hemel Hempstead,
Kings Langley and Rickmansworth. Ring your
local station to find out if there are any
restrictions on carrying bikes.

Distance: As far as you want. It is about
45 miles from Paddington to Marsworth.

NB. There is a short section of approximately
2 miles just north of Tring, between Tring
Summit at Bulbourne and Cow Roast Lock
(bridges 133 to 137), where cycling is prohibited
because the towpath is extremely narrow at this
point. You can easily work out a road alternative
that runs close to the canal if you take OS
Landranger Map Sheet 165 with you.

Maps: Ordnance Survey Landranger Sheets 165
and 166. The *Nicholson/Ordnance Survey Guide
to the Waterways
No. 1: South* is comprehensive.

Hills: None.

Surface: In general very good, at times
excellent. The towpath from London to Slough
is being improved.

Roads and road crossings: No dangerous road
crossings.

Refreshments:
(Pubs)
White Lion, Marsworth
Grand Junction Arms, Bulbourne
The Boat, Berkhamsted
The Three Horseshoes, Bourne End
The Fishery Inn, Boxmoor
The Albion, Hemel Hempstead
Dog and Partridge, Abbots Langley
Horse and Barge, Harefield
The Shovel, Cowley Lock
Turning Point, Cowley Peachey
General Elliott, Uxbridge
Black Horse, Greenford
Grand Junction Arms, Southall
Tea shop at Batchworth

Route Instructions:
No instructions are needed as it is difficult to lose something as big and as obvious as a canal! In deciding which stretches you may wish to do, take into account:
• your closest access point
• the proximity of a railway station to where you may want to start or finish

• whether you want to escape into the countryside (it starts to become much greener at Uxbridge)
• a 2-mile section of the towpath between bridges 133 and 137 (between Bulbourne, north of Tring and Cow Roast, northwest of Berkhamsted) is very narrow and cycling is prohibited.

Suggested sections to ride:

1. If you live within a couple of miles of the Grand Union in central and northwest London it is worth exploring the canal for its local interest and for the joy of cycling away from traffic so close to central London. It does tend to pass by factories, but sometimes there are compensations, such as the smells of baking bread and coffee (you pass close to the Nestlé factory).

2. Uxbridge marks the beginning of greener, less built-up areas. Uxbridge to Rickmansworth passes close to Denham Park and is a very pleasant 10-mile section near to London.

Tring reservoirs. *AA Picture Library*

THE NICKY LINE
(Between Hemel Hempstead and Harpenden)

This is a 5-mile ride along the course of
a dismantled railway line known as the
Nicky Line, although the reasons for the
name are a matter of dispute. Some say
that it derives from the half-length trousers
called 'knickerbockers', either because
the railway navvies wore such garments
or because the line was considered half-
size, being only single track. The name
may also have come from 'funicular',
referring to the exceptionally steep
gradients on the line, or even from
the parish of St Nicholas in Harpenden.

This is one of four short rides along
dismantled railways in Hertfordshire
which all lie close together.

The others are Routes 8, 9 and 10.

Background and Places of Interest

• **The London to
Birmingham Railway Line**
It was completed in 1838 and generated much
local interest in the network. A branch line was
proposed by the businessmen of Hemel
Hempstead to link the straw plait trade in the
town with the hat-makers of Luton. Thus the
Nicky Line was born and opened in 1877.
It carried passengers until 1947 and freight
until 1979.

• **St Albans**
Site of the Roman town of Verulamium.
There are remains of the walls, amphitheatre,
and the centrally-heated mosaic floors.
The Christian martyr St Alban was beheaded
on the hill where the cathedral now stands.

• **Whipsnade Zoo**
(10 miles northwest of Harpenden)
Open-air zoo on Dunstable Downs where
2,000 animals roam in the 500-acre park.
Rarities include a herd of white rhinoceroses.
Sea lions and other water mammals are
on display.

Facing Picture: Whipsnade Zoo. *AA Picture Library*

Starting Point: Park Hill, Harpenden.
Take the A1081 Luton road out of Harpenden.
Immediately after going under a railway bridge,
turn left on to Park Hill. Park 200yds up the hill,
just beyond a green metal gate on your left.

(You can also start from Hemel Hempstead
by following the B487 Redbourn/Harpenden
road out of town to the Eastman Way Industrial
Area. Just after passing the Site Z entrance to
Kodak on your right take the next left
signposted 'Nicky Line'. It is suggested you start
here only if you have arrived by bike as parking
may be difficult on the Trading Estate.)

Parking: As above.

Distance: 5 miles (10 miles round trip).

Map: Ordnance Survey Landranger Sheet 166

Hills: None.

Surface: Good, broad, stone-based track on the bed of a dismantled railway.

Roads and road crossings: Three busy roads to cross. Two at the roundabout of the B487 with the A5183 near Redbourn. The third road crossing is of the B487 near to the M1. Each of these roads may be very busy and extreme care should be taken if you are with young children.

Refreshments: None *en route*. Lots of choice in Harpenden.

Route Instructions:

1. At the roundabout where the B487 joins the A5183 you will need to cross two roads, aiming for a point diagonally right from where the cycle track joins the first road.

2. The route stops at the Trading Estate in Hemel Hempstead.

AYOT GREENWAY

(East from Wheathampstead, near Welwyn Garden City)

A short ride along the course of the old Luton, Dunstable and Welwyn Junction railway with some lovely wooded sections. If you enjoy this, there are three other rides on dismantled railways near by, described in Routes 7, 9 and 10.

Background and Places of Interest

Many men were employed in building the line, but the hardest workers would have been the navvies. A day's work for two of them would be to shovel 20 tons of rock and earth into 14 horse-drawn wagons. Although the work was hard, the pay, ranging between 15 shillings (75p) and 22 shillings and sixpence per week, was better than that of farm workers, so many men left the farms to work on the railway. It took two years to complete the stretch of line between Luton and Hatfield and the first excursion over the new section ran to London. The cheapest return fare from Luton to London was 2s 6d.

- **Ayot St Lawrence**
  (2 miles northeast of Wheathampstead)
  A peaceful village where George Bernard Shaw made his home, which has scarcely altered since his death in 1950. His typewriter still stands on a desk and his hats still hang in the hall.

- **Hatfield House**
  (6 miles south of Welwyn)
  Superb red-brick Jacobean mansion built in the early 17th century. Famous for its Marble Hall, Grand Staircase, Long Gallery and formal West Gardens. Tel: 0707 262823.

- **Knebworth House**
  (5 miles north of Welwyn)
  A stately home with Gothic towers and turrets and a Tudor Great Hall. Library doors masquerade as bookshelves. Set in 250 acres of formal gardens and deer park.

- **St Albans**
  (5 miles south of Wheathampstead) See route 9.

Starting Point: Free car park in Wheathampstead, just off the B651, 5 miles north of St Albans.

Parking: Turn off the main street in Wheathampstead by the Bull PH along East Street for 200yds.

Distance: 3 miles (6 miles round trip).

Map: Ordnance Survey Landranger Sheet 166.

Hills: None.

Surface: The section around the field edge close to Wheathampstead may be muddy after rain. Otherwise, good, broad, stone-based track.

Roads and road crossings: None.

Refreshments: In Wheathampstead; none along the route.

Route Instructions:

1. From the car park, return to the main street. Turn right and walk along the pavement for 100yds. Take the first right after the bridge on to Mount Road, signposted 'Public Bridleway Waterend 2¼' and bear left.

2. Follow this main path in the same direction passing through three gates and around a field edge (this section may be muddy after rain). At a T-junction with a broad gravel track, turn left under a bridge.

3. Climb the hill into a small wood. At a crossroads of broad gravel tracks, turn right through a wooden gate/barrier (signposted with a bicycle sign).

4. After 2.5 miles, descend some steps down to the road. It is suggested that you turn round and return at this point. The track does continue, but ends after 200yds at a small car park.

5. On your return, after 2.5 miles, turn left at the wooden barrier, go downhill and under the bridge. Shortly after the bridge, turn right on to the bridleway signposted 'Wheathampstead ½ mile'. Go through the housing estate and at the main street in Wheathampstead, turn left and left again by the Bull PH to return to the car park.

ROUTE 8
Ayot Greenway

WELWYN

B651

B653

Wheathampstead

A1 (M)

Steps

① ② ③ ④ ⑤ ⑥

Top: Hatfield House. *AA Picture Library* Bottom: Knebworth House. *AA Picture Library*

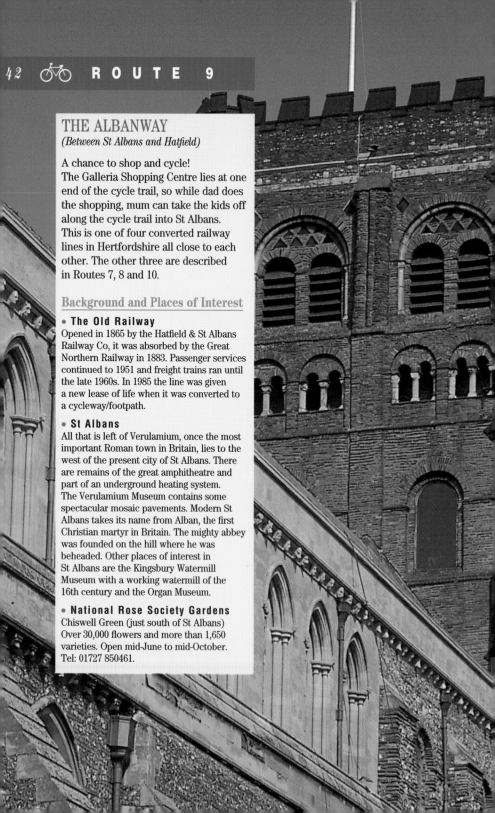

THE ALBANWAY
(Between St Albans and Hatfield)

A chance to shop and cycle!
The Galleria Shopping Centre lies at one
end of the cycle trail, so while dad does
the shopping, mum can take the kids off
along the cycle trail into St Albans.
This is one of four converted railway
lines in Hertfordshire all close to each
other. The other three are described
in Routes 7, 8 and 10.

Background and Places of Interest

• The Old Railway
Opened in 1865 by the Hatfield & St Albans
Railway Co, it was absorbed by the Great
Northern Railway in 1883. Passenger services
continued to 1951 and freight trains ran until
the late 1960s. In 1985 the line was given
a new lease of life when it was converted to
a cycleway/footpath.

• St Albans
All that is left of Verulamium, once the most
important Roman town in Britain, lies to the
west of the present city of St Albans. There
are remains of the great amphitheatre and
part of an underground heating system.
The Verulamium Museum contains some
spectacular mosaic pavements. Modern St
Albans takes its name from Alban, the first
Christian martyr in Britain. The mighty abbey
was founded on the hill where he was
beheaded. Other places of interest in
St Albans are the Kingsbury Watermill
Museum with a working watermill of the
16th century and the Organ Museum.

• National Rose Society Gardens
Chiswell Green (just south of St Albans)
Over 30,000 flowers and more than 1,650
varieties. Open mid-June to mid-October.
Tel: 01727 850461.

Starting Points/Parking:

1. St Albans, near the Abbey railway station. Follow the A5183 Radlett Road out of St Albans. At the traffic lights by the Abbey Theatre car park, just after a petrol station on the left but before the Abbey railway station, turn left on to Prospect Road. At the T-junction at the end of Prospect Road turn right and park near to the newsagents/stores. To get to the start of the railway path follow the road for 300yds, cross the railway bridge then turn immediately right and keep bearing right to go back under the bridge and join the railway path.

2. Hatfield. The Galleria Shopping Centre surface car park nearest to the Drive-In McDonalds at the back of the cinema complex. From Jct 3 of the A1(M) follow signs for Galleria then for A1001 Hertford. At the roundabout by the Peugeot dealer turn right signposted 'Galleria Parking' and bear left into the surface car park. Park at the far right-hand end near to the Drive-In McDonalds. To get to the start of the trail exit the car park and turn right alongside the decorative brick wall. Follow this road to its end, staying close to the wall, then climb the ramp/steps and turn right on to the tarmac path. Use the underpass, turn right, cross the bridge then turn left on to the railway path.

Distance: 4.5 miles (9 miles round trip).

Map: Ordnance Survey Landranger Sheet 166.

Hills: None.

Surface: Broad, stone-based or gravel track on the bed of the dismantled railway.

Roads and road crossings: Short sections on quiet roads at the start and finish. Three other road crossings (none are particularly busy).

Refreshments: In St Albans and Hatfield. None on the route.

Handy Tip: To get your bike through the many green metal barriers along the route, lift the handlebars up so that the bike is just on its back wheel and the handlebars are at chest height. You should be able to walk the bike through the gap.

Route Instructions:

1. Follow the railway path and cycle lane through St Albans. After almost 2 miles, descend to a road made of red bricks (Dellfield Road). Turn left, and cross to climb the steps opposite to rejoin the railway path.

2. Cross a second road near to the Fitness Connection Gymnasium then continue 2.5 miles into Hatfield. Use the underpass to cross to the Galleria.

St Albans Cathedral. *AA Picture Library*

(From Hatfield — see Starting Point and Parking above).

A. Exit the Galleria car park near McDonalds and turn right alongside the decorative brick wall. Follow this road to its end, staying close to the wall, then climb the ramp/steps and turn right on to the tarmac path. Use the underpass, turn right, cross the bridge then turn left on to the railway path.

B. Go through a housing estate. After 2.5 miles cross a road near to the Fitness Connection Centre.

C. Shortly, at a second road descend the steps, turn left then bear right and right again on to the continuation of the trail.

D. Follow for 2 miles to the end of the trail, beyond a new housing estate in St Albans.

Facing Picture: St Albans Cathedral. *AA Picture Library*

ROUTE 9

The Albanway

Galleria Shopping Centre

Cavendish Way

HATFIELD

Jct 3

A1 (M)

A414

Gym

A1081 London Road

steps

ST. ALBANS
Abbey
Railway Station

Dellfield Road

Below: Old railway lines make excellent cycle ways although not all are as well maintained as this one prepared by Sustrans. *Nick Cotton*

THE COLE GREENWAY
(West of Hertford)

Hertfordshire has four dismantled railways which have been converted to cycle trails; all are well maintained and pass through attractive woodland. None of them is particularly long, but it is from these small beginnings that local authorities piece together a whole network of leisure facilities for cyclists. This ride has perhaps the most rural feel of the four trails.

Background and Places of Interest

● The Cole Greenway
This follows the course of the old Hertford, Dunstable and Luton line. It was opened in 1858 by the Hertford & Welwyn Junction Railway and carried passengers up to 1951 and freight until 1962. It was acquired by Hertfordshire County Council in 1974 and converted to a walking and riding route.

● Hertford
Little remains of the old Norman castle except the lovely 15th-century gatehouse. This was one of the childhood homes of Elizabeth I. It was near to Hertford in 1712, in a village called Walkern, that the last trial for witchcraft ever held in England took place. As a result of the case, the barbaric laws relating to witchcraft were repealed.

● Paradise Wildlife Park
Broxbourne (5 miles south of Hertford) A lively leisure park and woodland zoo. Many attractions and a good variety of animals including lions, tigers, monkeys, camels and zebras. Woodland railway, crazy golf, souvenir shop, adventure playground, cafe and restaurant. Tel: 01992 468001.

Starting Points:
1. On the southeast edge of Welwyn Garden City. Follow the B195 towards Cole Green and Letty Green. At the start of the countryside at the edge of Welwyn Garden City turn right off the B195 signposted 'QE2 Hospital'. Park on either Holwell Hyde Lane or Holwell Hyde.

2. The Cole Greenway car park near the Cowper Arms in Cole Green. Turn off the A414 following signs for 'Cole Green/Birch Green' then for 'Letty Green'. The car park is just beyond the Cowper Arms PH on the left.

3. Hertford Town FC ground. Take the A414 out of Hertford towards Hatfield. Just after the Gates Ford garage turn left on to West Street signposted 'Hertford Town FC'. About 200yds after the end of the houses, on a left hand bend,

turn right by a bike sign down a tarmac lane leading to the car park.

Parking:
1. Cole Green. Turn off the A414 at Cole Green, signposted Letty Green. Just after the Cowper Arms PH, but before the bridge, turn left into the car park.

2. Hertford Town FC. Take the A414 out of Hertford towards Hatfield. Just after the Hartwells Ford Garage, turn left on West Street, signposted Hertford Town FC. About 200yds after the houses stop, on a left-hand bend, turn right by a lamp post down a tarmac lane.

Distance: 4.5 miles (9 miles round trip).

Map: Ordnance Survey Landranger Sheet 166.

Hills: None.

Surface: Good, broad, stone-based track on the bed of a dismantled railway.

Roads and road crossings: None

Refreshments: The Cowper Arms PH at Cole Green.

The Black Horse PH in Hertford, just beyond the end of the cycleway.

Route Instructions:
(From Welwyn Garden City)
1. Follow the trail for just over 4 miles. Near to the the vast, brick railway viaduct in Hertford bear right on the main track then at a T-junction of tracks turn left to pass beneath the arches to emerge in Hertford Football Club car park.

(From Hertford)
2. From the car park at the football club take the track that leads towards the left-hand end of the railway arches. After going under the arches, take the first right by a white gate. Continue for 4.5 miles as far as the B195 at the edge of Welwyn Garden City.

ROUTE 10

Cole Greenway

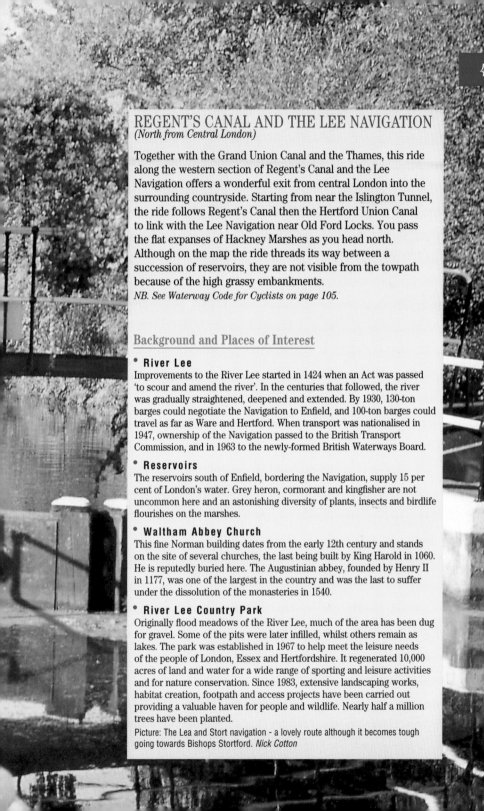

REGENT'S CANAL AND THE LEE NAVIGATION
(North from Central London)

Together with the Grand Union Canal and the Thames, this ride
along the western section of Regent's Canal and the Lee
Navigation offers a wonderful exit from central London into the
surrounding countryside. Starting from near the Islington Tunnel,
the ride follows Regent's Canal then the Hertford Union Canal
to link with the Lee Navigation near Old Ford Locks. You pass
the flat expanses of Hackney Marshes as you head north.
Although on the map the ride threads its way between a
succession of reservoirs, they are not visible from the towpath
because of the high grassy embankments.
NB. See Waterway Code for Cyclists on page 105.

Background and Places of Interest

• River Lee
Improvements to the River Lee started in 1424 when an Act was passed
'to scour and amend the river'. In the centuries that followed, the river
was gradually straightened, deepened and extended. By 1930, 130-ton
barges could negotiate the Navigation to Enfield, and 100-ton barges could
travel as far as Ware and Hertford. When transport was nationalised in
1947, ownership of the Navigation passed to the British Transport
Commission, and in 1963 to the newly-formed British Waterways Board.

• Reservoirs
The reservoirs south of Enfield, bordering the Navigation, supply 15 per
cent of London's water. Grey heron, cormorant and kingfisher are not
uncommon here and an astonishing diversity of plants, insects and birdlife
flourishes on the marshes.

• Waltham Abbey Church
This fine Norman building dates from the early 12th century and stands
on the site of several churches, the last being built by King Harold in 1060.
He is reputedly buried here. The Augustinian abbey, founded by Henry II
in 1177, was one of the largest in the country and was the last to suffer
under the dissolution of the monasteries in 1540.

• River Lee Country Park
Originally flood meadows of the River Lee, much of the area has been dug
for gravel. Some of the pits were later infilled, whilst others remain as
lakes. The park was established in 1967 to help meet the leisure needs
of the people of London, Essex and Hertfordshire. It regenerated 10,000
acres of land and water for a wide range of sporting and leisure activities
and for nature conservation. Since 1983, extensive landscaping works,
habitat creation, footpath and access projects have been carried out
providing a valuable haven for people and wildlife. Nearly half a million
trees have been planted.

Picture: The Lea and Stort navigation - a lovely route although it becomes tough
going towards Bishops Stortford. *Nick Cotton*

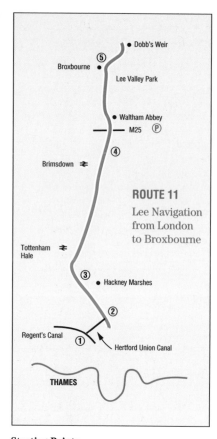

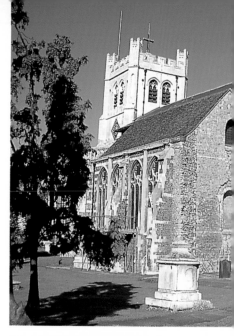

ROUTE 11

Lee Navigation
from London
to Broxbourne

Maps: Ordnance Survey Landranger Sheets 166 and 176. *The Nicholson Guide to the Waterways (South)* is a comprehensive guide to this and other canals in Southern Britain. Leaflets with maps of the Lee and Stort Navigation are produced by British Waterways and are available by sending an SAE to: British Waterways, The Toll House, Delamere Terrace, Little Venice, London W2 6ND.
Tel: 0171-286 6101.

Hills: None.

Surface: The Lee Navigation towpath has recently been improved and is wider, better surfaced and less busy with pedestrians than Regent's Canal or the Hertford Union Canal.

Roads and road crossings:
None of significance.

Refreshments:
Narrowboat PH, St Peters Street, Islington, near to start. The Overdraught PH, Dunston Street, Haggerston; Royal Cricketers PH, SW corner of Victoria Park; Prince of Wales PH, Ship Aground PH, Clapton (Hackney Marsh); Robin Hood PH, Anchor and Hope PH, High Hill Ferry, Clapton; Cafe at Stonebridge Lock; Cooks Ferry Inn, Edmonton; Greyhound PH, Rifles PH, Enfield Lock; The Crown PH, Broxbourne; Fish and Eels PH, Dobb's Weir.

Bike Hire: Available from Easter to September from Lee Valley Cycle Hire, Mill Lane, Broxbourne Meadows, next to Model Railway Club. Tel: 01992 630127.

Starting Points:

1. The corner of Danbury Street and Graham Street near Angel tube station, Islington

2. Victoria Park, Hackney

3. Waltham Abbey

4. The following railway stations are close to the Lee Navigation: Hackney Wick, Clapton, Tottenham Hale, Northumberland Park, Angel Road, Ponders End, Brimsdown, Enfield Lock, Waltham Cross, Cheshunt, Broxbourne (all served from Liverpool Street). There are often special family fares available. For further information, telephone 0345 484950.

Parking:
Victoria Park, Hackney.
Pickett's Lock Recreation Centre.
Waltham Abbey (Highbridge car park).
Broxbourne.

Distance: 18 miles from the Islington Tunnel to Broxbourne.

Above: Waltham Abbey. *AA Picture Library*

Route Instructions:

1. Two miles from the start of the canal towpath at the Islington Tunnel, at the corner of Victoria Park, by the Royal Cricketers PH and just before the paved section ends, leave Regent's Canal and join the Hertford Union Canal.

2. After a mile, at the junction of the Hertford Union Canal and the Lee Navigation, cross the metal bridge and turn left on to the towpath heading north out of London, signposted 'Hackney Marshes'. Remember this point for the return trip.

3. After the Anchor and Hope PH at High Hill Ferry there are towpaths on both sides of the canal. Stay on the left-hand side.

4. Go past several pubs and cafes, changing sides as necessary. Pass beneath the M25 just before the Old Englishman PH in Waltham Abbey.

5. In Broxbourne you will need to cross the canal via a green metal bridge by the Crown PH. It is suggested that you go only as far as the Fish and Eels PH at Dobb's Weir as the surface deteriorates shortly beyond this point.

Nick Cotton

A CIRCUIT IN EPPING FOREST

A circular ride through one of the green lungs to the north of London. The tracks are broad and well maintained and the old oak and beech trees are a real delight.

Please note that there are several roads running through Epping Forest so take care with children at road crossings. The ride could easily be linked with the Lee Navigation through Lee Valley Park, north of Waltham Abbey.

Background and Places of Interest

• Epping Forest

This is one of Europe's oldest forests, a labyrinth of footpaths and bridleways covering some 6,000 acres. It owes its creation to the Norman Conquest. It was maintained as a royal hunting area through the reigns of various monarchs and in the reign of King Charles I its bounds were fixed to embrace some 60,000 acres. In 1882 what was left of it was formally opened as a publicly owned area by Queen Victoria.

• Queen Elizabeth's Hunting Lodge

(at the southern end of Epping Forest).
A wood and plaster building thought to have been erected towards the end of the 15th century so that the monarch of the day could enjoy a grandstand view of the chase. Having served as a keeper's lodge for a number of years, it now houses the Epping Forest Museum.

Starting Point and Parking: Take the A104 Epping road out of London towards Epping. At the roundabout by the Robin Hood PH, turn left for 200yds on to the High Beach road and park in the first car park on the left.

Distance: 9 miles.

Map: Ordnance Survey Landranger Sheet 167.

Hills: Several short, steep hills.

Surface: Quite a variety, ranging from stone-based gravel tracks to hard earth tracks. Expect some mud after rain and in winter.

Roads and road crossings: Several minor lanes are crossed and five fairly busy roads — the A121 (twice) the B1393, the B172 and the A104.

Refreshments: The Robin Hood PH The City Limits Bar. There is also a tea hut in the car park where you start.

Route Instructions:

1. Leave the car park and turn left on to the main road (towards High Beach) for 70yds then right through a metal barrier marked 'Emergency Access' on to a track.

2. Follow the main track. At the first road, turn right then left through a metal barrier, 'Emergency Access'. At a second road, go straight across 'Emergency Access'. Ignore a left turn after 150yds.

3. You will arrive at the next road, the busy A121, near a bus stop. Take care, crossing straight ahead between wooden posts, then shortly, at a T-junction of tracks, turn right.

4. Just before the track rejoins the road (near the roundabout with the City Limits Bar), with a tall wooden fence ahead of you, fork left.

5. Cross a minor road. The next section is noisy, running parallel with the B1393. Take care crossing this busy road then go straight ahead through a metal barrier 'Emergency Access'.

6. After 300 yds, at a T-junction of tracks, near to a clump of silver birch trees on your right, turn right. Go through car parks either side of the B172.

7. After less than 0.5 mile, take the first, broad, fine gravel track to the right. Go down and up a steep hill, through another car park. Take care crossing the busy A121. Go through a metal barrier marked 'Emergency Access'.

8. Follow another steep downhill stretch, then

go up, through a car park, and cross the road by a pond. Continue straight ahead through the emergency access barrier.

9. Easily missed! After 0.5 mile, on a gentle descent, shortly after passing a grass clearing on the left with a black and white timbered house in the distance turn right on to a broad track. Cross the busy A104 then turn right at the first minor road and climb back up to the starting point.

53

Queen Elizabeth's Hunting Lodge. *AA Picture Library*

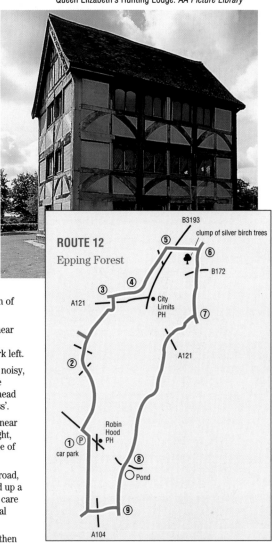

ROUTE 12

Epping Forest

THE KENNET AND AVON CANAL TOWPATH

(Between Newbury and Reading at Aldermaston)

In the summer of 1997 the canal authority introduced a £12.50 yearly permit (free for under 16s). This is available from British Waterways, Bath Road, Devizes SN10 1HB (Tel: 01380 722859) or can be purchased from the Visitor Centre at Aldermaston. One can only hope that the money generated from these permits will lead to a considerable improvement in this section of the towpath which at present compares very badly with the Grand Union Canal, the Lee Navigation, the Thames Towpath and the Basingstoke Canal (all described elsewhere in the book) and the much better-maintained western end of the canal.

See the Waterway Code for Cyclists page 105.

Background and Places of Interest

• Kennet and Avon Canal

Completed in 1810, the canal became an important link between the major sea port of Bristol and River Thames at Reading, forming the only waterway across southern England and connecting other canals from Somerset through to Oxford and the north of England. The canal flourished for a while but settled into slow decline from the mid-19th century onwards with the development of the railways.

Starting Point: Aldermaston Wharf, just off the A4, halfway between Theale (Junction 12 on the M4) and Thatcham.

Parking: As above.

Distance: 1.5 miles northeast from Aldermaston Wharf to Ufton Bridge (3 miles round trip).

2 miles southwest from Aldermaston Wharf to the Rowbarge PH at Woolhampton (4 miles round trip).

Maps: Ordnance Survey Landranger Sheets 174 and 175. The GEOprojects map of the

By 1952 an application for its closure was submitted to parliament. This was opposed by the Kennet and Avon Canal Association and in the next 35 years they raised almost £3 million to restore the 87-mile waterway, including the replacement of 344 lock gates! In August 1990 the Queen officially reopened the canal at a ceremony in Devizes.

NB. Should you wish to join the Kennet and Avon Canal Trust please write to: The Kennet and Avon Canal Trust, Canal Centre, Couch Lane, Devizes, Wiltshire. SN10 1EB (Tel: 01380 721279) for an application form.

• The Visitor Centre, Aldermaston Wharf

Canal exhibition and information centre with a picnic garden and limited refreshments. Also a canal souvenir/gift shop, a nature trail and an historical trail. Toilets. Open Monday to Saturday, 10.00am-5.00pm. Tel: 01734 712868.

• Beale Bird Park

(8 miles north of Aldermaston Wharf, between Pangbourne and Goring)

Flamingos, peacocks and a fine collection of ornamental pheasants share this meadowland reserve beside the Thames. Boat trips, riverside walks, craft centre and adventure playground.

• Silchester

(6 miles southeast of Aldermaston Wharf)

Rich wool-trading town in Roman times called Calleva Atrebatum. Unusual in that almost all the other sites of Roman towns in Britain have become towns in their own right, whereas all that remains of Silchester is a 2-mile section of wall and the site of the amphitheatre. Calleva Museum displays Roman pottery and other exhibits.

Kennet and Avon Canal contains a wealth of information and is available by sending £4.25 to GEOprojects Ltd, 9-10 Southern Court, South Street, Reading RG1 4QS. Tel: 0118 939 3567.

Hills: None.

Surface: Narrow track, at times rutted and overgrown. As explained in the introduction, it is hoped that the revenue raised from the cycling permits will lead to a drastic improvement in the state of the towpath, both in its surface and the width that is free of vegetation.

ROUTE 13

Kennet and
Avon Canal at
Aldermaston Wharf

READING

A4

Aldermaston Wharf   Ufton Bridge

BATH
                          (P)
                          START
                          Kennet and Avon Canal
Row Barge PH

A340

Roads and road crossings: One road crossing
needs care: the A340 to the west of the starting
point. No sections on roads.

Refreshments:
At the Canal Centre at Aldermaston Wharf.
The Rowbarge PH at Woolhampton. The Butt
Inn, 100yds along the A340.

Route Instructions:
Very simple! If you wish to cycle the 1.5 miles
to Ufton Bridge, turn LEFT along the canal
towpath. If you wish to visit the Rowbarge PH
at Woolhampton, turn RIGHT for 2 miles.

Basildon Park Gardens. *AA Picture Library*

THEY MOVE · THEY SPEA

WINDSOR GREAT PARK

The park is a self-contained world almost frozen in time. There is an estate village with a village shop, fields are ploughed, seeded and harvested, there are woods and lakes and a school and yet the M3, M4 and M25 are only a couple of miles away and Heathrow 5 miles away.

This circuit around the park provides fine views of the castle and down the Long Walk and the chance to see a polo match if you happen to come on the right day. And then there's the big gate that opens with the push of a button...

AA Picture Library

Background and Places of Interest

• **Windsor Great Park**
The remnant of a royal hunting forest with ancient oaks, herds of deer, and polo matches most summer weekends.

• **Savill Garden**
Famous for its rhododendrons; the Valley Garden is noted for heathers. Near by is the artificial 160-acre lake of Virginia Water. (Please note that there is no cycling around Virginia Water.)

• **Windsor Castle**
Established by William the Conqueror, it is the largest inhabited castle in the world. The enormous round tower has a view over 12 counties.

Starting Point: The Bishop's Gate Entrance to Windsor Great Park, on the east side of the park, 2 miles south of Old Windsor (off the A328 which links the A30 and the A308).

Parking: There is some parking beyond the Fox and Hounds PH, near to Bishop's Gate itself. If all the spaces here are taken, follow signs for Savill Garden car park and join the route near Cumberland Gate.

Distance: A 5-mile circuit plus two side trips of 3 and 4 miles, one of which goes to Blacknest Gate (passing the polo grounds and crossing a creek of Virginia Water), the other to the end of Duke's Lane at Prince Consort's Gate. Both of these spurs lead to main roads, which is why it is suggested that you turn back at the end of each side trip on reaching the edge of the park.

Map: Ordnance Survey Landranger sheet 175, or maps of the park (20p) are available at the ticket office to the Savill Garden.

Hills: A gentle 100-ft climb from Virginia Water back towards Bishop's Gate.

Stockfile

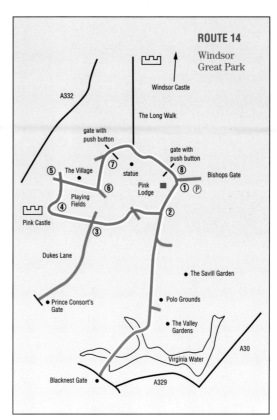

Surface: All tarmac. Within Windsor Great Park cycling is not allowed on anything other than tarmac roads, several of which are in fact out of bounds (signs will tell you where you cannot go).

Roads and road crossings: All the route is on very lightly trafficked roads. They may be slightly busier if there is a polo match on. The roads tend to be very open with good visibility so vehicles should not be a danger.

Refreshments:
Cafe/restaurant at Savill Garden.

The Village Shop (signposted) sells what you would expect in a small village shop.

Route Instructions:
1. From Bishop's Gate, go towards the large pink lodge house. Turn left at the junction of roads just in front of the pink house, signposted 'Royal School, Royal Collection Stores, Cumberland Lodge'.

2. After 0.5 mile take the first right (*) signposted 'Royal School', then take the second of two closely spaced roads to the left 'Royal School'.

(* or go straight ahead for the polo grounds at Smith's Lawn, Virginia Water, and Blacknest Gate).

3. After 0.5 mile, at a crossroads with a red-brick house called 'The Hollies' to the left, go straight ahead (or turn left here 'Commercial vehicles prohibited' for a side trip to the edge of the park at Prince Consort's Gate).

4. After 0.75 mile, at the pink castle, turn right.

5. Take the first right at the crossroads just past the playing fields and ponds, signposted 'The Village'.

6. Go through the village. About 300yds past the last house on the left, take the next left at a crossroads.

7. Push the button so that the gates open for you. Pass by the top of the Long Walk and exit by another set of gates.

8. At the crossroads by the pink lodge house, turn left for Bishop's Gate.

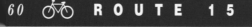

ROUTE 15
Basingstoke Canal

Wey Navigation (see Route 16)

M25

LONDON Ⓟ

Woking

A322

Deepcut Locks

Frimley Green

Jct 5   M3
Crookham
A325 A321
Greywell   Fleet   Ash
Ⓟ   Aldershot
Odiham   Coxmoor Wood

Starting Points:

1. Odiham Wharf car park, Odiham.

2. Fleet, just off the B3013 by the traffic lights at the bridge over the canal.

3. Frimley Lodge Park between Frimley and Mytchett.

4. Woking, Brewery Road car park.

5. West Byfleet Railway Station car park.

Parking: As above.

Distance: 32 miles between Greywell (west of Odiham) and the junction with the River Wey Navigation near West Byfleet. The 15-mile Surrey section from Aldershot towards London has the best quality surface, and the section between Woking and Deepcut is one of the prettiest stretches.

Maps: Ordnance Survey Landranger Sheet 186 covers 95 per cent of the route (it runs on to Sheet 187 between West Byfleet and Weybridge). Alternatively, the GEOprojects map contains a wealth of information and covers the whole canal in one map. Available by sending £3.50 to: GEOprojects Ltd, 9-10 Southern Court, South Street, Reading RG1 4QS. Tel: 0118 939 3567.

Hills: None.

Surface: Stone or packed earth track in Hampshire, at times a bit rough, particularly along a short stretch in Coxmoor Wood, west of Fleet, where there are still traces of concrete Second World War defences. Very good quality broad gravel track on the Surrey section (soon after the lock at Ash).

Road crossings: Very few for such a long stretch in this built-up area. One at Ash Lock, north of Aldershot. Four more in the Surrey section, often involving a change in side for the towpath. Care should be taken, although none of the roads crossed are on fast stretches.

Refreshments:
Barley Mow Antiques Tea Shop, Barley Mow PH, near Odiham The Chequers PH, Fox and Hounds PH, Crookham Beavers Bar PH, Kiln Bridge, Woking. Bridge Barn PH, Woking Potters PH, Mytchett Kings Head PH, near Deepcut

Route Instructions:
Follow the canal! The route changes sides with some frequency on the Surrey section, so be prepared for this. It is possible to link the Basingstoke Canal to the Thames Towpath via the Wey Navigation between West Byfleet and Weybridge and thus form a continuous waterside route from Putney Bridge to Odiham, a distance of over 50 miles (see details on page 65).

THE BASINGSTOKE CANAL
(Between Odiham and Weybridge)

One of the best traffic-free exits from London into the countryside (from the Thames Towpath via the Wey Navigation on to the Basingstoke Canal). The western end of the canal is surrounded by woods and farmland. Between Fleet and Brookwood, much of the canal is bordered by military-owned heathland. A wide variety of trees grow along the banks, giving the canal a delightful feeling of seclusion, even in built-up areas. The flight of locks between Woking and Deepcut is one of the loveliest sections of the whole canal.NB. *See the Waterway Code for Cyclists page 104.*

Background and Places of Interest

• The Basingstoke Canal
This was finally completed in 1794. It was 37 miles long with 29 locks and a 1,230-yd tunnel through Greywell Hill. The canal was built to boost agricultural trade in central Hampshire, carrying coal and fertilizers from London, returning with timber, corn and other produce to the capital. The canal was never a commercial success, although there were a succession of plans to extend the canal and create a continuous inland waterway between London and the major ports of Southampton, Portsmouth and Bristol.

The canal was auctioned in 1950 for £6,000. By the mid-1960s the canal was lying semi-derelict. All the locks were decaying, the towpath was overgrown and the water channel choked by weed, refuse and silt. Efforts to stop the rot were made by the Surrey and Hampshire Canal Society, formed in 1966. But it took a seven-year campaign for public ownership before serious work began. Restoration work was completed and the canal reopened in 1991.

• King John's Castle, North Warnborough
Built by King John as a hunting lodge. He rode from the castle to Runnymede in 1215 to seal Magna Carta.

• Frimley Lodge Park
(between Frimley and Mytchett)
A 60-acre park with woodland and a children's adventure playground.

• Deepcut Locks, Pirbright
A flight of 14 locks, spread over a distance of 2 miles, raises the canal by 100ft on to the Great Heath.

Nick Cotton

THE THAMES TOWPATH
(Between Putney Bridge and Weybridge)

The Thames towpath is one of the best exits from the southwest of London, with plenty of places of interest to see along the way. There is a striking contrast between the wide, untamed tidal stretch as far west as Teddington Lock and the highly managed pleasure-boat section which lies beyond. If you were feeling very adventurous, you could link this route with the Basingstoke Canal via the Wey Navigation at Weybridge and end up more than 50 miles later in Odiham, in deepest Hampshire! At the London end, it would be easy to link Wimbledon Common and Richmond Park to the route. Please note that the towpath may be busy with pedestrians, particularly on summer weekends, so please slow down, be courteous and show consideration.

Background and Places of Interest

• **The Thames**
London owes its existence to the Thames and to the bridge the Romans built in the 1st century AD. The Thames was both a corridor for ocean-going shipping (from before the Romans arrived until as recently as 30 years ago) and also a barrier between the land to the south and north which needed bridging. London's geology provided the firm base needed to support bridge structures.

The river is tidal as far as Teddington Lock where its character changes dramatically, becoming much neater and picturesque to the west of this point.

• **Kew Gardens**
Royal Botanic Gardens begun in 1759 when Princess Augusta, mother of George III, had a private garden laid out. It now covers 300 acres and has more than 25,000 species and varieties of plant with royal buildings, statues, glasshouses and an 18th-century pagoda.

• **Syon Park**
Laid out by Capability Brown in the 18th century, it includes the Great Conservatory, a rose garden and a butterfly house.

• **Hampton Court Palace**
Built by Cardinal Wolsey in the early 16th century who later gave it to Henry VIII in a vain attempt to curry favour. It became one of the king's favourite residences and he often played Real Tennis or practised jousting here. Five of his wives lived here and the ghosts of two (Jane Seymour and Catherine Howard) are said to haunt it. The intricate gardens, with their famous maze, were added by Charles II and are reminiscent of Versailles.
Tel: 0181-781 9500.

The Thames at Chiswick. *Stockfile*

Hampton Court. *AA Picture Library*

Starting Point: At any point along the River Thames between Weybridge (near Shepperton Lock) and Putney Bridge (near the Star and Garter PH). The towpath runs along what is easiest to describe as the southern side of the river for all but a short section between Hampton Court Bridge and Kingston Bridge, where it runs on the northern side.

Parking: Some parking at the far end of Embankment Road beyond the Star and Garter PH just off Lower Richmond Road, west of Putney Bridge. Car parks at north end of Kew Gardens, Kingston, on Ham Lands opposite Eel Pie Island, Richmond and by Walton Bridge, Walton-on-Thames.

Trains: There are stations near the river at Hampton Court, Kingston upon Thames, Twickenham, Richmond, Kew Bridge, Mortlake and Barnes Bridge. Some of these are up to 0.5 mile from the river and it would be as well to take a copy of *London AZ* with you. Telephone the station before you go, to check if there are restrictions.

Distance: 24 miles in total. Factors to bear in mind when deciding which section to do are that busy roads need to be crossed (via pedestrian crossings) at Kingston and Hampton Court bridges and that there is a short rough stretch between Chiswick and Barnes Bridge.

Map: The OS Landranger is not much help. Better to use a coloured AZ map in book or fold-out map form.

Hills: None.

Surface: Excellent, all-year round, broad gravel track. There is a short stretch of 200yds between Chiswick and Barnes Bridges (near to Young's Brewery) that is occasionally flooded after very high tides, so this section may be a bit muddy.

Roads and road crossings: Two, one at Kingston Bridge and one at Hampton Court Bridge where the towpath changes sides. These are both busy roads, but both have pedestrian crossings at the northern end of the bridges. In the case of Hampton Court Bridge it is best to walk away from the river as far as the pedestrian crossing, cross the road and walk back along the opposite pavement over the bridge to rejoin the towpath on the southern side.

Refreshments:
The Weir PH, The Anglers PH, Walton. Lots of choice in Kingston and Richmond; The Ship PH, Mortlake; The Star and Garter PH, Putney

Route Instructions:

You will need to cross the river at Kingston. Dismount and walk the bike past the shops and restaurants and beneath the bridge. Turn left and left again, walk the bike along the pavement to cross the bridge and rejoin the towpath. At Hampton Court Bridge, walk towards the roundabout (away from the river), cross the road via the pedestrian crossing then walk back along the pavement across the bridge to regain the towpath. Remember these bridge crossings for your return.

NB. There is a short section along the towpath near Richmond Bridge where it is necessary to dismount and push your bike.

Thames to Wey Navigation link (and Basingstoke Canal)

If you wish to continue beyond Weybridge, the Thames towpath becomes very bitty. You may prefer to follow the Wey Navigation to join the Basingstoke Canal (see page 60). The following instructions link the two waterway systems.

1. Follow the Thames westwards from Walton Bridge for 1.5 miles. At the end of the broad gravel track, with a large weir away to your right, continue beyond a barrier and small car park/layby on to the road past the Lincoln Arms

PH. At the Old Crown PH, turn right past public conveniences, cross a metal bridge and bear right at a fork on to a narrow track (there is a gate to the left) to cross a hump-backed bridge over the Wey Navigation. Remember this section for your return.

2. Follow this for 2.5 miles, eventually crossing beneath the noisy M25. At this point the waterways fork: turn right for the Basingstoke Canal (signposted 'Greywell 31').

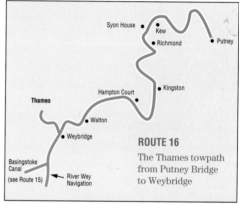

ROUTE 16

The Thames towpath from Putney Bridge to Weybridge

Below: Kew Gardens, the new conservatory. *AA Picture Library*

ROUTE 17

Wimbledon Common and Richmond Park

East Sheen Gate

Richmond Gate

Telegraph PH

Putney Heath

②

Richmond Park

Pen Ponds

③

A3

Robin Hood Gate ⑧

Windmill ●

Ⓟ ① Windmill Road

④

Pembroke Lodge Cafe

Ham Cross

⑨

Kingston Vale

⑦

⑤ Wimbledon Common

Ham Gate

⑥

Kingston Gate

Camp Road

WIMBLEDON COMMON, PUTNEY HEATH & RICHMOND PARK

This ride links two of the largest green lungs in the southwest of London. Wimbledon Common consists of 1,045 acres of natural heath and Richmond Park has 2,400 acres of plantations and heath, plus some very fine deer. The recently completed Tamsin Trail around the perimeter of Richmond Park is one of the best things to have happened to leisure cycling in London for many years.

Background and Places of Interest

- **The Windmill Museum, Wimbledon Common**
Built in 1817 and used for grinding corn, it is now a museum of windmill history. Open 2.00-5.00pm Saturday and Sunday from April to October.

Picture: Richmond Park. *AA Picture Library*

Windmill, Wimbledon Common. *Nick Cotton*

Starting Points and Parking:

1. The windmill car park on Wimbledon Common, at the end of Windmill Road, off Wimbledon Parkside.

2. Any of the car parks near the gates/entrances into Richmond Park.

Distance: There are about 5 miles of cycle trails through Wimbledon Common. The Tamsin Trail around Richmond Park is 8 miles long.

Map: Ordnance Survey maps do not show enough detail within London. Either use a large-scale, coloured AZ map or you could send an SAE, requesting a map, to:

1. Ranger's Office, Wimbledon and Putney Conservators, Wimbledon Common, London SW19.

2. Royal Parks, Richmond Park, Richmond, Surrey TW10 5HS. Tel 0181 948 3209.

Hills: Gentle hill in Richmond Park.

Surface: Good stone-based or gravel tracks, or tarmac.

Roads and road crossings: Several quiet roads are crossed. The busy A3 is crossed via underpasses from Wimbledon Common to Putney Heath. The route from Wimbledon

Common to Richmond Park crosses the A3 via a footbridge then has one busy road (the A308 Kingston Vale) to cross near Robin Hood Gate.

Refreshments: There is a cafe at Pembroke Lodge on the west side of Richmond Park.

Route Instructions:
1. (North from the windmill) From the Windmill car park go back to the tarmac lane then turn left opposite the large metal spin wheel on to a track at the end of the grass traffic island by a green metal barrier/gate (bike sign). Ignore two right turns signposted 'No Cycling' then bear right at the next fork. Follow signs for Roehampton through the underpass beneath the A3, turning sharp left back on yourself at the end of the second underpass.

2. Go past the Telegraph PH, over the crossroads with Wildcroft Road then take the next left on to Portsmouth Road.

3. Go back underneath the A3, following this broad track in the same direction, ignoring turnings to the right and left to return to the windmill.

4. (South from the windmill into Richmond Park) From the Windmill car park go back to the tarmac lane then turn right alongside a wooden fence towards a green metal barrier.

5. Follow this main track as it curves round to

the right. Bear right at a fork by a white metal barrier then right again at the junction with a tarmac lane, passing a low white cottage, and crossing a car parking area towards a broad, descending track.

6. At the bottom of the descent, just before a bridge over the brook, turn right and follow this track parallel to the brook out of the woodland.

7. Just before the red-brick pavilion turn left over the bridge and across the field towards the footbridge over the A3. Cross the footbridge then TAKE CARE crossing the A308 (Kingston Vale). Turn right then left to enter Richmond Park.

8. The broad, gravel Tamsin Trail around the perimeter is easy to follow. It is described here in a clockwise direction, ie enter the park and turn left (although you could just as easily do it anti-clockwise!). The signboards at each gate will indicate where you are. Go past Kingston Gate, then at Ham Gate, where a small pond lies ahead and an ornate white house lies to the left outside the gates, turn right uphill alongside the road then turn left at the crossroads at the top of the hill

9. Go past Pembroke Lodge (cafe and gardens), Richmond Gate, East Sheen Gate and then a golf course on your left to return to Robin Hood Gate.

Mottisfont Abbey. AA Picture Library

SOUTH FROM STOCKBRIDGE
(Along the Test Way near Winchester)

This 5-mile section of the Test Way south from Stockbridge runs parallel with and occasionally crosses the delightfully clear, shallow, fast-flowing River Test — one of the best fishing rivers in England. The old railway track has been converted into a good, broad, stone-based trail, wide enough to cycle side by side and have a chat! The only drawback is that there is no connection from the end of the track to Mottisfont Abbey except via a short stretch of the very busy A3057.

Background and Places of Interest

• The Test Valley Railway Line
Also known as the 'Sprat and Winkle' line, it was unusual in that it was built on the bed of an old canal which linked Andover and Southampton. The waterway was first used in 1794 but had fallen into disuse within 50 years. The railway began service in 1865 and was much used in both World Wars to move troops and supplies to Southampton Docks. It closed in 1964 and has since become part of the Test Way, a long-distance footpath from Inkpen to Totton. Short sections of it are open to cyclists.

• Stockbridge
People come from all over the world to fish the Test, one of the most sought-after game rivers in the country. Stockbridge itself is a one-street town of mainly 19th-century buildings.

• Mottisfont Abbey
(near the southern end of the ride)
A National Trust house converted from a medieval monastery where all is not what it seems: painted illusions by Rex Whistler include ornamental plasterwork and alcoves. There are cedar trees in the romantic, walled rose garden.

• Farley Mount Country Park
(5 miles southeast of Stockbridge)
The Roman road from Winchester to Salisbury cuts through the downs in this 1,000-acre park. There are rare plants, waymarked woodland walks, a prehistoric burial ground and fine views from the 572-ft Beacon Hill.

• Winchester
Royal capital of Saxon Wessex, and of England until the late 12th century. The fine medieval Great Hall is all that remains of the castle begun in 1067 and rebuilt by Henry III. The cathedral dates from the 11th century and is the second longest in Europe. Inside are coffins holding the bones of Saxon kings.

Starting Point: Trafalgar Way, next to the White Hart PH, at the roundabout at the eastern end of the High Street, Stockbridge.

Parking: Where you can along Stockbridge's long, broad High Street, bearing in mind that the ride starts near the roundabout at the junction of the A3057, the A272 and the A30.

Distance: The cycle track runs 5 miles south from Stockbridge to the Stony Marsh car park near the A3057 (10 miles round trip).

Maps: Ordnance Survey Landranger Sheet 185.

Hills: None.

Surface: Good, broad, gravel track.

Roads and road crossings: One quiet lane at Horsebridge. If you wish to visit Mottisfont Abbey you will either have to spend a short time on the very busy A3057 or leave the cycle track at Horsebridge and make your way there on the quiet lane that runs parallel to the River Test.

Refreshments:
Lots of choice in Stockbridge The John of Gaunt PH by the River Test at Horsebridge.

Route Instructions:
1. Once you have found the start of the track at the end of Trafalgar Way near the White Hart PH, you should have no difficulty following it for the next 5 miles.

2. If you wish to cycle to Mottisfont Abbey, it would be better to leave the cycle track at the John of Gaunt PH at Horsebridge, turn RIGHT and use quiet lanes to get there rather than brave the horrendous traffic of the A3057 which lies at the end of the cycle track.

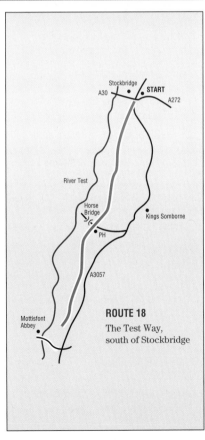

ROUTE 18

The Test Way, south of Stockbridge

WEST MEON TO WICKHAM

A good 10-mile stretch of dismantled railway running through the heart of Hampshire. Lots of fine wooded sections, deep chalk cuttings and, just off the route itself, some wonderful refreshment stops. It is surprising that Hampshire does not blow its own trumpet more about this route (no leaflet has been produced and no signposts put up) as it is one of the best stretches of flat, vehicle-free cycling in this part of the world.

Background and Places of Interest

• Wickham
Georgian houses of red and grey brick surround the square. The mill next to the bridge was built from timbers of the American frigate Chesapeake, captured in 1813.

• West Meon
An old village with timbered cottages and gabled roofs. It is the burial place of Thomas Lord, founder of Lord's cricket ground in London. The nearby village of Hambledon was the early home of cricket: the cricket club (founded in 1760) evolved the laws of modern cricket.

• Mid Hants Railway
Best known as the Watercress Line, this steam railway runs along 10 miles of the old Winchester to Alton line between Alresford and Alton. The trains travel through beautiful Hampshire countryside with views of hills and the watercress beds that gave the line its nickname. At Ropley several steam locomotives are being restored.
There are special events throughout the year.

Starting Points: West Meon, Droxford, Wickham.

Parking:
1. West Meon. Follow the A32 southwards out of West Meon towards Fareham. Go past the Red Lion PH on your right. After 150yds, on a sharp right-hand bend, turn left on to Station Road signposted 'single track with passing places', then take the first lane/track on the right. There are lots of places to park near the start

of the ride. Warning: there is a height barrier at the entrance to the car park so do not go through if you have bikes on a roof rack!

2. Droxford. Near the church. To join the cycle track, walk uphill from the church/bus shelter/telephone box in the centre of the village and take the first tiny lane on the right (Mill Lane). Follow this downhill, past the houses alongside the stream then across the bridge. At the main road, turn right and right again just

before the bridge to go up on to the cycle track.

3. Wickham. From the main square in Wickham, follow Free Parking signs out of town towards the A32. About 150yds after leaving the square, turn left on to Mill Lane, then first right by the fire station on to Station Close and right again to park beneath the trees. Follow the broad tarmac drive/track.

Distance: 6.5 miles between Wickham and Droxford. 3.5 miles between Droxford and West Meon.

Maps: Ordnance Survey Sheets 185 and 196.

Hills: None.

Surface: Good, broad, gravel track. It may get slightly muddy after rain or in the winter.

Roads and road crossings: No busy road crossings or road sections.

Refreshments:
Red Lion PH, Thomas Lord PH, West Meon White Horse PH, The Hurdles PH, Droxford White Lion PH, Soberton Kings Head PH and more choice in Wickham

Route Instructions:
Once you are on the cycle track, it is very easy to follow. Getting to the start can sometimes be a little more difficult, and knowing where you are at any given time is also a test of your map reading skills. A short tarmac stretch and a view of the Hurdles PH from a bridge indicates that you are in Droxford.

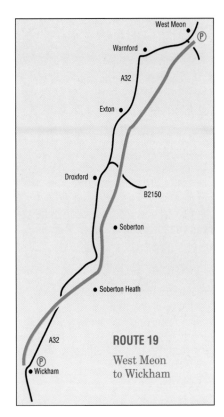

ROUTE 19

West Meon
to Wickham

(map labels: West Meon, Warnford, A32, Exton, Droxford, B2150, Soberton, Soberton Heath, A32, Wickham)

Left: Railway bridge near Wickham. *Nick Cotton*
Above: ath between Droxford and West Meon. *Nick Cotton*

DOWNS LINK

Each of these two routes follows sections of the Downs Link, the bridleway following a dismantled railway which connects the North Downs at Guildford with the South Downs near the South Coast.

Route 20a South from Cranleigh to the Thurlow Arms PH or Slinfold

This section has been chosen because the surface is generally good and the track broad and stone-based. The area is heavily wooded. The Thurlow Arms at Baynards Station is a convenient refreshment stop. It is worth doing this ride in May when the woods south of the Thurlow Arms are carpeted with a magnificent display of bluebells.

Background and Places of Interest

- **Downs Link**
The original railway was built in two stages: the first in 1861 by the London, Brighton & South Coast Railway from the coast to Christ's Hospital, the second in 1865 by the Horsham and Guildford Direct Railway Company from Christ's Hospital to Guildford. Neither line achieved the glory hoped for by the builders and after a century of use, both railways fell to the Beeching Axe in 1966.

- **The two-tiered bridge near Rudgwick**
This unusual bridge over the Arun gives the Downs Link its logo. The higher bridge was built because the railway inspector disliked the steep gradient to Rudgwick station. (You will need to descend from the route into the woods to appreciate it.)

Picture: Nick Cotton

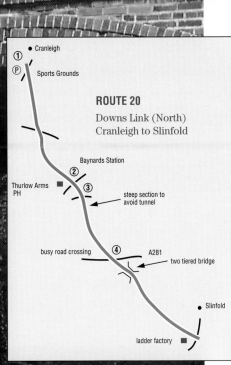

ROUTE 20

Downs Link (North)
Cranleigh to Slinfold

Cranleigh
Sports Grounds
Baynards Station
Thurlow Arms PH
steep section to avoid tunnel
busy road crossing
A281
two tiered bridge
Slinfold
ladder factory

Starting Point and Parking: The main car park in Cranleigh, the entrance of which is near to the ornate clock in Stocklund Square and the National Westminster Bank in Cranleigh's main street. Park in the furthest corner to be near to the start of the track.

Distance: 3.5 miles from Cranleigh to the Thurlow Arms PH; a further 4 miles to Slinfold.

Map: Ordnance Survey Sheet 187.

Hills: None as far as the Thurlow Arms PH. One short steep hill beyond the pub.

Surface: Broad, stone or gravel track. There may be some large, unavoidable, muddy puddles after wet weather and in the winter.

Roads and road crossings: One road crossing near the start in Cranleigh. If you go on to Slinfold, there is one very busy road to cross (the A281). The last 0.5 mile into Slinfold is on a quiet lane.

Refreshments:
Thurlow Arms PH, Baynards
King's Head PH, Slinfold

Route Instructions:

1. Exit at the corner of the car park and turn left. After 300yds, cross the road towards the houses then shortly turn right by low wooden posts, signposted 'Downs Link'. Follow the track/lane between playing fields. Continue for 3.5 miles to the Thurlow Arms PH.

2. (If you are going beyond the Thurlow Arms PH to Slinfold.) At a tarmac lane just beyond the pub, turn left then right, signposted 'Downs Link'.

3. NB. Remember this next section for the return trip. Just beyond the first bridge, turn left uphill on to the road, cross the bridge then go first left through a gate signposted 'Public Bridleway. Downs Link'. In order to avoid the old tunnel, you now have a steep climb. After 400yds, at a crossroads of tracks, turn left on to the Downs Link and go steeply downhill. A short muddy stretch follows.

4. EXTREME CARE. You have to cross the busy A281. The surface is much better on the other side of the road.

5. 200yds after passing a ladder and scaffolding factory on your right, turn left to go into Slinfold.

Retrace your route back to the start, taking care to remember the section to avoid the tunnel (route direction 3).

20b Southwater Country Park to Partridge Green or Henfield

This is another section of the Downs Link. The stretch which is missed out, between Slinfold and Southwater, is the least enjoyable part of the Downs Link, hence the new starting point. Along here the vistas begin to open up, particularly at the southern end, with the whaleback ridge of the South Downs looming on the horizon. There are good stopping points at the pub at Partridge Green or by the River Adur south of Henfield, which is a good spot for a picnic.

Background and Places of Interest

• Southwater Country Park
Opened in June 1985 by Horsham District Council, the park provides some 54 acres for informal recreation and conservation. It is open from dawn to dusk each day and now features a visitor centre close to the Downs Link (open at weekends from April to October). There are refreshments in the centre. The site used to be a brickworks, home of the Southwater Red Engineering Brick. Around 1,000 million of these bricks were produced during the factory's working life from 1890 to 1981.

• Winkworth Arboretum
(5 miles northwest of Cranleigh)
Wide open spaces with views over the North Downs. Nearly 100 acres of hillside cloaked with azaleas and bluebells, rare trees and shrubs. There is also a lake. Best seen in spring and autumn.

ROUTE 20

Downs Link (South)
Southwater to the
River Adur
near Henfield

Starting Point: Southwater Country Park, just off the A24 south of Horsham.

Parking: As above.

Distance: 5 miles from Southwater to Partridge Green. Another 3.5 miles to the River Adur beyond Henfield.

Map: Ordnance Survey Landranger Sheet 198.

Hills: None.

Surface: Broad, stone or gravel track as far as Partridge Green. One grass field to cross south of Partridge Green.

Roads and road crossings: To get to the Partridge PH at Partridge Green you have to cross the B2135, which can at times be busy. If you continue beyond Henfield you will need to spend 0.5 mile on the reasonably busy B2135 south of Partridge Green. There is a short stretch on a quiet lane in Henfield.

Refreshments:
Bridge House PH, 1 mile south of Southwater. Partridge PH at Partridge Green Cat and Canary PH in Henfield.

NB. The section north from Southwater to

Slinfold is the least pleasant stretch of the Downs Link. There are several gates, a long road section, narrow, overgrown, muddy stretches and a blind bend to cope with!

Route Instructions:
1. Exit the car park towards the road by a wooden post near to the car park entrance. Cross the road on to Stakers Lane 'Copsale, Horsham'. Cross the road into Stakers Lane, signposted 'Downs Link'.

2. Go under the noisy A24. As the tarmac track swings left by a red-brick building (water treatment works), bear right by a wooden fence, soon joining a good broad track. After 0.5 mile cross a minor lane by the Bridge House PH.

3. Four miles after the Bridge House PH, at a crossroads with a broad tarmac lane, you should be able to see the yellow-hatted tree trunk creature in the garden of the Partridge PH. Go straight ahead for continuation of the route or turn left here for the pub.

4. At the T-junction with the road (the B2135) turn right. Ignore the first left to the Star Trading Estate. Take the next tarmac lane to the left signposted 'Bridleway, Downs Link'. At a crossroads of tracks after 400yds turn right.

5. Cross a field on a narrow track.

6. There is a short climb to a small gravel car park on the road by the Cat and Canary PH. At the road, turn left then first right, opposite the pub. After 200yds, as the road swings to the left, turn right on to Hollands Lane then left on to the Downs Link. You may wish to stop for a picnic at the river. Turn round at this point and return to the start.

Nick Cotton

THE WORTH WAY
(West of East Grinstead)

A 5-mile ride along the course of a dismantled railway west from East Grinstead towards Crawley. East Grinstead has become a large and busy commuter town but it is amazing how quickly you can escape from the noise and traffic into the wooded avenue that forms the Worth Way. There is a short section in the middle of the route where you need to use roads to go through Crawley Down, but you soon return to the woodland once again.

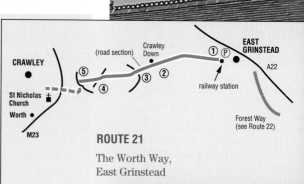

ROUTE 21

The Worth Way, East Grinstead

Background and Places of Interest

• Branch Line
The 7-mile branch line between Three Bridges and East Grinstead was opened in 1855 and continued operating for over a century until 1966, when the whole stretch from Three Bridges through East Grinstead to Groombridge was closed. The line was purchased by West Sussex County Council in 1977.

• St Nicholas Church
Worth's parish church is an Anglo-Saxon church dating back 200 years before the Norman Conquest.

• Bluebell Railway
(6 miles south of East Grinstead)
Steam engines run along the 5-mile line between Horsted Keynes and Sheffield Park. There is a collection of locomotives and rolling stock dating from between 1865 and 1958.

Bluebell Railway. *AA Picture Library*

Starting Point and parking: The car park is at the back of the railway station in East Grinstead. Follow the one-way system out of town on the A22 (A264) towards London and Crawley. After passing the railway station on your left, just before a major junction with the A264 Tunbridge Wells road, turn left on to Park Road, then first left on to Grosvenor Road. Turn right into the station car park. The Worth Way starts by a wooden signpost on the right.

Distance: 6.5 miles (13 miles round trip).

Map: Ordnance Survey Landranger Sheet 187.

Hills: None.

Surface: Good, broad gravel track. There may be muddy puddles after rain or in winter.

Roads and road crossings: Several crossings of quiet lanes. Short section through a housing estate at Crawley Down.

Refreshments: No obvious pubs. Picnic possibilities by the lake near Crawley Down.

Route Instructions:

1. The trail starts by a wooden marker post on the right hand edge of the car park to the right of the entrance.

2. After 2.5 miles, join tarmac soon after the pond/lake to the east of Crawley Down. You are aiming to continue in the same direction but housing estates have been built on the course of the old railway, hence the following instructions:

At the T-junction at the end of Cob Close, turn left signposted 'Worth Way'. At the T-junction at the end of Hazel Way, turn right. At the T-junction at the end of Woodland Drive, turn left. At the crossroads at the end of Burleigh Way, by the Royal Oak PH, go straight ahead on to a No Through Road — Old Station Close.

3. Tarmac turns to track. At the first road, go straight ahead on to a continuation of the track.

4. At the second road, by a brick and slate building, turn left then shortly right through Rowfant car park.

5. The railway path ends at the third road (by Keepers Cottage) but it is possible to continue a further mile to the church at Worth on a good, stone-based bridleway. Cross the road and turn left on to the track along the verge. On a sharp left-hand bend after 200yds turn right and follow this track in the same direction for a mile, past a farm and over the M23 as far as Worth.

Worth Way (see route 21)

East Grinstead   Ⓟ
①

②

   A22

③   ● Forest Row

ROUTE 22

The Forest Way,
East Grinstead

Groombridge
(Crown PH)

④

B2110

Hartfield
(Winnie the
Pooh country)

THE FOREST WAY
(East Grinstead to Groombridge)

A fine ride through woodland and arable land along the course of a dismantled railway between East Grinstead and Groombridge. There are picnic tables along the way and the broad, good-quality track makes an ideal ride for combined exercise and conversation! The ride could easily be linked with the Worth Way, the other route from East Grinstead (see page 78).

Background and Places of Interest

• Railway Line
The line was opened by the London, Brighton & South Coast Railway in 1866 as an extension of the Three Bridges to East Grinstead branch line. Forest Row was the busiest of the intermediate stations dealing in minerals and general goods. The railway was absorbed into the Southern Railway Co in 1923. It was finally closed as part of the Beeching cuts in 1966.

• Coppiced Woodlands
Between East Grinstead and Forest Row there are signs of sweet chestnut and hornbeam coppice. Coppicing is a traditional woodland management technique whereby the trees are cut near their base so new shoots are formed, producing wood suitable for fencing. In the past the wood was also used for hop poles and iron smelting.

• Oasthouses
An oasthouse is a kiln for drying hops and these distinctive buildings are reminders that a large area of East Sussex was formerly a hop garden. The hops were spread out on a perforated floor of wooden battens. Special hearths at ground level below created hot air which rose through the hops and out through the roof, which was equipped with a rotating cowl to improve the draught. The hops were then cooled, pressed, packed into sacks and transported to the brewery.

• Hartfield
The countryside around Hartfield is the setting of A. A. Milne's Winnie the Pooh stories.

Starting Point and Parking: The car park is on College Lane/De La Warr Road on the east of East Grinstead, on the town centre side of the roundabout on the A22 Eastbourne Road.

Distance: 9 miles (18 miles round trip).

Maps: Ordnance Survey Landranger Sheets 187 and 188.

Hills: None.

Surface: Good, broad gravel track.

Roads and road crossings: Getting to the start of the ride from the car park involves a short distance on quiet roads then crossing one busy road. After 3 miles you will have to cross the busy A22. This needs care. If you wish to visit the pubs below you will have to spend a short time on roads.

Refreshments: Three excellent pubs all just off the route — the Anchor at Hartfield, the Dorset Arms at Withyham and the Crown at Groombridge.

Route Instructions:
1. From the car park return to De La Warr Road and turn right. At the T-junction with College Lane turn right for 100yds then first

Top and bottom left: *Stockfile*

left downhill by a stone wall.

2. At the end of Old Road, cross to the pavement on the other side, with care. Turn left along the pavement and shortly turn right through the fence on to a path leading downhill. Follow this to the road. Cross the road on to Forest Way.

3. At the A22 you will have to go down some steps. Take great care crossing here and continue straight ahead on to a tarmac track signposted 'Tablehurst Farm'. After 400yds, shortly after passing Forest Row Pumping Station on your left, near the end of a line of cypress trees turn right by a post marked with a blue arrow.

4. After almost 4 miles, at a T-junction, just after going through a large yellow stone bridge under the B2026, turn left then right past Hartfield Station, which is now a private house.

5. The Forest Way cycle track ends after a further 2.5 miles at the B2110 just to the west of Groombridge. You arrive at this road shortly after descending a set of wooden steps. If you wish to continue to the Crown PH, turn left along the road for 1.5 miles. If not, retrace your steps.

Cissbury Ring. *AA Picture Library*

STEYNING BOWL TO CHANCTONBURY RING

(North of Worthing)

One of the series of rides that use short sections of the ridge of the South Downs Way. This one has as its goal Chanctonbury Ring, the distinctive copse of tall beech trees that was decimated by the great storm of 1987. There are signs of regrowth although it will be at least a hundred years before the copse regains its former majesty. This notwithstanding, the area is very atmospheric and the views are magnificent.

Background and Places of Interest

• The South Downs
Stretching west from Beachy Head into Hampshire, the South Downs range is all that remains of a huge chalk backbone that connected England with the Continent until about 6,000 years ago.

• Chanctonbury Ring
The extensive prehistoric earthworks occupy a 783-ft downland summit which affords views over some 30 miles of countryside. The original beeches were planted in 1760 by Charles Goring of Wiston House. There are many traditions associated with the Ring, which add to its mystical qualities.

• Cissbury Ring
(3 miles north of Worthing, just off the A24)

Impressive Iron Age hillfort covering 60 acres, built about 300BC. The site was previously used by Stone Age man to mine flints. Burial mounds remain.

• Bramber
(just east of Steyning)
A gaunt tower on a moated hill is all that remains of the days when this village was a Norman stronghold.

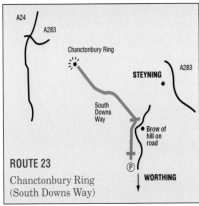

ROUTE 23
Chanctonbury Ring
(South Downs Way)

Distance: 4.5 miles (9 miles round trip).

Map: Ordnance Survey Landranger Sheet 198.

Hills: A 550ft climb from the car park to Chanctonbury Ring. This could be reduced to 300ft if the driver leaves his/her passengers at the road's highest point (near to the private car park), drives down to the public car park then rejoins them by bike.

Surface: Good, broad, countryside track.

Roads and road crossings: The road can be busy, particularly in summer. You may wish to climb up to Chanctonbury Ring on tracks then use the road for 1 mile on your descent back to the car park..

Starting Point and Parking: The car park is at Grid Reference 163080 on the minor road between Sompting (near Worthing) and Steyning. The minor road is signposted from the south end of Steyning 'Sompting via Bostal'. The car park lies 2 miles north of the A27, on the west side of the road (on the left going up, on the right going down), halfway up/down the hill, with broad stone tracks going off to either side, opposite a 'Sompting' sign. NB The car park at the brow of the hill, marked on the Ordnance Survey map at GR163095, is private and not open to the public.

Route Instructions:
Take the track away from the road on the same side as the car park. Descend to a crossroads of tracks and turn right uphill, climbing steeply then steadily. Continue in the same direction, following signs for South Downs Way to the distinctive clump of trees at Chanctonbury Ring. On your return/descent, either retrace your route OR, at the point where you are nearest to the road, leave the track and go back downhill on tarmac to the car park.

DITCHLING BEACON
(North of Brighton)

The middle one of the three rides that use sections of the South Downs ridge.
In addition to the magnificent views one expects from the top of the Downs, this one has the added attraction of a visit to the Jack and Jill windmills above Clayton.

Background and Places of Interest

• Jack and Jill Windmills
Noted Sussex landmarks: 'Jack' is a brick-built towermill of 1866. 'Jill' is a wooden postmill, built in Brighton in 1821 and dragged to Clayton in about 1850 by a team of oxen. It has recently been restored and is open on Sundays in summer.

• Clayton
(West of Ditchling)
The Tunnel House, a 19th-century folly, was built in the shape of a Tudor fortress when the railway was excavated under the Downs and includes the tunnel-keeper's cottage.

• Ditchling
Village best known for the 16th-century Anne of Cleves' house. Other treasures in the narrow streets include an old candlemaker's workshop and the 17th-century red-brick Old Meeting House where dissenters gathered.

• Devil's Dyke
(6 miles southwest of Ditchling)
A naturally formed deep and dry grassy moat on the downs with a hillfort above. According to legend, the Devil dug the dyke to flood the Weald with the English Channel and frustrate the growth of Christianity.

• Lewes
(7 miles southeast of Ditchling)
The county town of East Sussex on a steep hill overlooking the River Ouse. The medieval streets are crammed with fine buildings of all periods. The town is surmounted by a Norman castle.

• The Bluebell Railway
(10 miles to the north on the A275 towards East Grinstead)
Steam engines run on a 5-mile line between Horsted Keynes and Sheffield Park, where there is a period railway station and a museum housing a collection of locomotives and rolling stock dating between 1865 and 1958.

Foxgloves on the South Downs. *Nick Cotton*

Starting Point:
Ditchling Beacon car park situated 6 miles north of Brighton. Turn off the A27 near the University.

OR, 5 miles south of Burgess Hill, take a combination of the B2112 and B2116 into Ditchling then follow signs for Ditchling Beacon.

Parking: As above.

Distance: 3 miles east to Black Cap (6 miles round trip) and 2 miles west to the Jack and Jill windmills (4 miles round trip).

Map: Ordnance Survey Landranger Sheet 198.

Hills: Gently downhill to the east, so a gentle climb to return to the car park. A longer descent

ROUTE 24

Ditchling Beacon
(South Downs Way)

of 260ft to the windmills so it is a climb to return to the start.

Surface: Good, firm, broad countryside tracks. One slightly rough section near the windmills.

Roads and road crossings: Take care crossing the road by the car park.

Refreshments: In Ditchling.

Route Instructions: 1. If you wish to go east to Black Cap, carefully cross the road and follow the South Downs Way for 3 miles.

2. If you wish to visit the Jack and Jill windmills, do NOT cross the road, follow the South Downs Way from the back of the Car Park for 3 miles.

ROUTE 25

Firle Beacon
(South Downs Way)

Lewes

A27

West Firle

P

Firle Beacon

South Downs Way

Bostal Hill

A26

River Ouse

Alfriston

Starting Point: The car park on top of the downs, off the A27, 5 miles east of Lewes, signposted Firle Beacon.

Parking: As above.

Distance: You can go 2 miles to the east or west without dropping too much height, remaining on the wonderful ridge (ie both are round trips of 4 miles).

Maps: Ordnance Survey Landranger Sheets 198 and 199.

Hills: (East from the car park) A 190-ft climb from the car park to the top of Firle Beacon. If you go on to Bostal Hill you will have another 160-ft climb back to the Beacon on your return.

(West from the car park) A 100-ft climb to the masts. If you go on to the trig point, you will be faced with an 80-ft climb back to the masts.

Surface: Good, broad, well-drained track, at times grassy. It should be passable all year round but you may well encounter some mud after heavy rain or in the winter.

Roads and road crossings: None.

Refreshments: Ram Inn PH in West Firle

Route Instructions:

1. Going east towards the beacon, leave the broad stone track. Follow the large Footpath sign through the gate into the field and aim for the hill ahead. You can either come straight

FIRLE BEACON
(Along the South Downs between Lewes and Eastbourne)

The most easterly of the three rides that use sections of the South Downs ridge; it would be easy to do all three in a day. As with the other South Downs Way rides, there are magnificent views in all directions, out to sea and down into the Weald of Sussex and Kent. You may well see paragliders and hang gliders taking off from the hillside, too. Alternatively, you might consider trying out the nearby rides from Exceat into Friston Forest and the Seven Sisters Country Park.

Background and Places of Interest

• Firle Place
The home of the Gage family since the 15th century. The original Tudor manor house was largely altered in about 1730. Impressive art collection including works by Rubens. Open May to the end of September Sundays, Wednesdays and Thursdays, 2.00-5.00pm. Cream teas from 3.00pm.

• Drusillas Zoo Park
(just off the A27 towards Polegate)
Apart from the zoo itself, there is a great variety of other attractions: a butterfly house, a bakery selling its own freshly baked bread, an adventure playground and a railway to take passengers on a round trip through the park. Near by is the English Wine Centre and Wine Museum.

• Lewes
The county town of East Sussex on a steep hill overlooking the River Ouse, crammed with fine buildings of all periods, medieval streets and Georgian houses, surmounted by a Norman Castle. Traditionally, every 5 November the streets throng with torchlit processions and bonfires blaze in celebration of Guy Fawkes.

Left: Lewes Castle. *AA Picture Library*
Inset: St Peters Church, Firle. *AA Picture Library*

back from the beacon or go on to the next hill, or, if you are feeling incredibly energetic, go right down into Alfriston. The return journey involves over 850ft of climbing altogether.

2. If you are going west towards the masts, the climb is not so long or steep. It is suggested that you go only as far as the trig point but if you are feeling super fit you can always go right down into the valley of the River Ouse and come back up again (650ft of climbing).

NB. It is only worth descending into the river valleys on mountain bikes. You are likely to damage bikes which are less robustly built.

Facing Picture: *Stockfile*

EXCEAT TO THE COAST & INTO FRISTON FOREST

Only four rivers cut through the chalk of the South Downs to the coast: the Arun, the Adur, the Ouse and the Cuckmere. These two short rides start where the Cuckmere has cut a broad gap through the chalk near the sea. Both are remarkably flat for what is predominantly very hilly country. The ride through the forest is just a suggestion: the land is owned by the Forestry Commission and has an open access policy on the hard roads within the forest.

Background and Places of Interest

• Friston Forest
This extends over 2,000 acres of chalk downland, most of which is planted with trees. Planting began in 1926 and the aim of the forester has been to establish a largely broadleaf forest, primarily beech. As Friston Forest is only a mile from the sea, exposure to salt-laden winds is severe. Beech saplings have been protected by using pines to 'nurse' them over the first 25 years.

• Smuggling
The Sussex Coast has always proved popular with smugglers. In the 1800s they ran their contraband inland from Cuckmere Haven across the Downs to Jevington and Alfriston where they had hideouts. They were often assisted by local farmers who ran their sheep across the smugglers' tracks to obliterate them.

• Seven Sisters Country Park
The Visitor Centre is housed in a converted 18th-century barn at Exceat Farm. The Living World is a mini-zoo of small creatures including butterflies, bees, spiders, scorpions and marine life. Open Easter to October 11.00am-5.30pm daily and for the rest of the year at weekends only, 11.00am-4.00pm.

• Alfriston
A carefully preserved village in the Cuckmere Gap with a 14th-century church and Clergy House. The 15th-century Star Inn has a ship's figurehead. A very place busy at weekends and in the summer.

• Drusillas Zoo Park
See page 87

The Clergy House, Alfriston. *AA Picture Library*

Cuckmere Valley. *AA Picture Library*

Starting Point: The car park at Exceat on the A259 between Eastbourne and Seaford.

Parking: As above (there are two car parks here, one on the coast side and one on the forest side of the road).

Distance: 1 mile to the coast. A 4.5-mile waymarked trail in the forest.

Map: Ordnance Survey Landranger Sheet 199.

Hills: None to the coast. One short climb in the woodland, at times steep.

Surface: Concrete or gravel to the coast. Good forest tracks in the woodland; both rides can be attempted all year round.

Roads and road crossings: Take extreme care when crossing the A259. Best to cross between

the telephone box and the bike-hire centre.

Refreshments: At the bike-hire centre.

Cycle Hire: Available from the Cuckmere Cycle Co Ltd, Friston Forest, next to Exceat Farmhouse. Tel: 01323 870310.

Route Instructions:
(To the coast)
Facing towards the sea, take the broad concrete track to the left of the car park (by the bus stop, signposted 'To the beach, Foxholes'). After 0.75 mile, as the main concrete track swings left towards Foxholes, bear right on to a gravel track. Fine sea views.

(Waymarked forest route)
1. Start at the entrance to the first car park on the right on the minor lane leading away from

the A259 towards Litlington and Wilmington (signposted 'Country Park/Living World'). Turn immediately left through the car park to the start of the family cycle trail by the wooden 'claws' sculptures.

2. Go past a flint house called Pond Cottage. After a mile go past two more flint buildings on the left. At a crossroads of tracks go straight ahead. Follow the main track around a left-hand bend then shortly turn left uphill on to an earth track by a metal barrier and soon turn left again on to a grassy track.

3. At a T-junction with a wide stone forestry track turn right then take the first forestry road to the left. Climb steeply then half way down the descent turn left on to a grassy track. At a T-junction with a wide stone forestry track turn right to rejoin the outward route back to the start.

ROUTE 26
Friston Forest

THE CUCKOO TRAIL
(Hailsham to Polegate)

This is one of the longest stretches of top-quality dismantled railway in the southeast of the country, and there are plans for extensions both to the south (to Eastbourne) and to the north (towards Mayfield). This has come about as a result of a happy joining of forces between the local authority, Wealden District Council, and Sustrans. There are many fine and interesting sculptures in metal and wood along the trail. The whole project shows what can be achieved where there is sufficient impetus and resources to pursue a good idea.

Background and Places of Interest

• The Cuckoo Line
The railway line from Polegate to Eridge was named The Cuckoo Line by the railwaymen because of a Sussex tradition that the first cuckoo of spring was released each year at Heathfield Fair. The railway opened in 1880 and ran until 1968. It was bought by the local authorities in 1981, but little was done for the first ten years. Then a joint venture between Wealden District Council and Sustrans, a charity specialising in building cycle paths on disused railways, was set up to reconstruct the whole route as a high-quality path for walkers and cyclists.

• Pevensey Castle
(5 miles east of Polegate)
A mighty Roman fort, already old when William the Conqueror landed on Pevensey Beach in 1066. The Normans built a powerful stone fortress, still impressive with walls 12ft thick. The nearby Mint House is where Norman coins were produced.

• Brightling
(7 miles east of Heathfield)
Strange obelisks, domes, towers and a peculiar cone known as the Sugar Loaf are scattered around this quiet village. They are all follies of 19th-century eccentric 'Mad Jack' Fuller, local squire and MP. He was buried under a churchyard pyramid 60ft high. Local legend claims that he sits in top hat and tails holding a bottle of claret!

Pevensey Castle. *AA Picture Library*

Brighting Church and Jack Fuller's grave. *AA Picture Library*

Starting Points: Heathfield, Hailsham or Polegate.

Parking:

1. Heathfield. Turn off the High Street, opposite Barclays Bank, on to Station Road. Take the second right on to Newnham Way then turn immediately left into the car park.

2. Hailsham. Follow signs for Eastbourne A295 (A22). Follow South Road as it bears left, then, just past Hailsham Free Church on your right, take the next left into a car park.

3. Polegate. From the intersection of the A22 and A27, just north of Polegate, take the A27 east towards Pevensey. After 0.5 mile, shortly after passing Polegate railway station on your right, turn left signposted 'Cuckoo Trail, Hailsham, Heathfield'. After 300yds turn left on to Windsor Way and park along here. Retrace your steps for 100yds to get to the start of the Cuckoo Trail.

Distance: 3.5 miles from Polegate to Hailsham.

7.5 miles from Hailsham to Heathfield.

Map: Ordnance Survey Landranger Sheet 199.

Hills: The railway climbs almost 300ft from Polegate to Heathfield, so it is best to start at Polegate and do the uphill gradient while you are fresh.

Surface: A mixture of tarmac and fine quality gravel track.

Roads and road crossings: Several road crossings, mainly on quiet roads. The busiest road (the B2104) has traffic lights which make crossing safer. The route through Hailsham uses a short section of road, but there is a broad pavement alongside if you wish to walk and avoid the traffic.

Cycle Hire: Cuckmere Cycle Co Ltd at Horam. Tel: 01435 813000

Refreshments: There are pubs and tea shops in Heathfield and Hailsham.

Route Instructions
(going north from Polegate):

1. The start north from Polegate is easy to follow.

2. In Hailsham, at the end of Freshfield Close, turn right on to Lindfield Drive, then at a T-junction with a larger road, with the pond ahead, turn left for 300yds. (Walk along the pavement if you wish to avoid the traffic.) Just past the Railway Tavern PH on your right, turn left into the car park. Go diagonally left through the car park and under the bridge to continue the route.

3. Continue going north, in the same direction, through a couple of small housing estates. Follow the signposts.

4. You will eventually finish the Cuckoo Trail at a small gravel car park in Heathfield. Turn right and at the T-junction turn left uphill if you want to go into the centre of Heathfield.

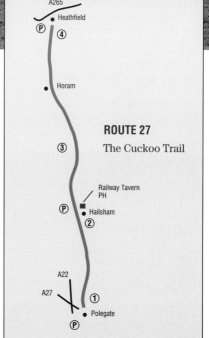

ROUTE 27
The Cuckoo Trail

BEWL WATER
(Southeast of Tunbridge Wells)

A circular route around the largest reservoir in the southeast of the country. This is one of the few circular rides in the book and the setting is lovely. However, compared to cycle trails around other reservoirs in the country, such as Grafham Water (see page 20) or Rutland Water and the Derwent Reservoirs (described in the 'Midlands and the Peak District' book in the series) the standard of the surface of the trail leaves much to be desired, and it is impassable (and closed to cycling) in winter. Choose a fine day after a dry spell, however, and you should have few problems!

Background and Places of Interest

• The Dam
Made from local clay and faced with concrete slabs to prevent erosion, the dam holds back 6,900 million gallons of water. The tall draw-off tower controls water abstraction. Nearby Chingley Wood is a mixed coppice woodland once used for fuelling ironworks in the valley.

Several willow plantations around the lake produce timber for the manufacture of cricket bats.

• The Floating Fish Farm
Located to the west of the Visitor Centre, this rears 50,000 rainbow and brown trout every year which are used to stock the lake.

• Woodland Adventure Playground
Forts, a huge slide and the House of the Three Bears.
Cruise around the lake aboard the SS Frances Mary, a beautifully restored wooden passenger boat that runs from April to October.

• Lamberhurst
Ancient centre of the local iron industry. Now a vineyard grows besides the village green. There are ingenious displays in Heaver's Model Museum and Craft Centre in a converted oast house. Smugglers used Owl House and warned of approaching excisemen by hooting.

• Scotney Castle
(1 mile north of Bewl Water)
Romantic landscaped gardens awash with roses and flowering shrubs set around the moated ruins of a 14th-century castle.

Nick Cotton

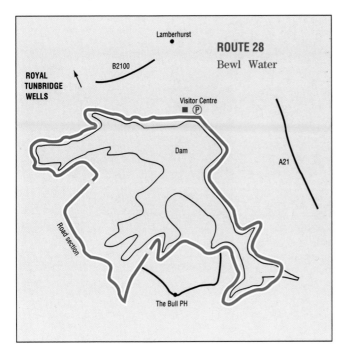

Lamberhurst

ROUTE 28

Bewl Water

B2100

ROYAL
TUNBRIDGE
WELLS

Visitor Centre

Dam

A21

Road section

The Bull PH

Tel: 01860 386144.

Route Instructions:
The route starts from
the back of the brick
building housing the
cafe, opposite the
terrace. The route is
waymarked with
'Round Water Route'
signs but the
waymarking is
patchy and it is not
sufficient to say
'follow the edge of
the lake' as the route
veers away from the
water's edge on the
southern part of the
ride. On the tarmac
sections, keep an eye
out for 'Round Water
Route' signs at each
junction.

NB. In its entirety, as
a circuit, this ride is
one of the toughest
in the book because
of the poor quality of
many of the tracks. These will get much
muddier after wet weather (the route is shut
during the winter), so bear this in mind when
deciding on footwear and calculating how long
it may take you. Should you feel like writing a
letter with your views, please address it to: The
Amenity and Recreation Manager, Bewl Water,
Lamberhurst, Tunbridge Wells, Kent TN3 8JH.

Starting Point: The Visitors Centre,
Bewl Water, near Lamberhurst, off the A21
between Tunbridge Wells and Hastings.

Parking: At the Visitors Centre.

Distance: 12.5 miles.

Map: Ordnance Survey Landranger Sheet 188.

Hills: Several short climbs. One longer climb
(on road) of 170ft on the south side of the lake.

Surface: Varied. There are
sections of tarmac, good gravel
track, firm earth track, and
some rough, rutted and at
times muddy stretches. Avoid
this route after prolonged rain.
It is closed in winter.

Roads and road crossings:
The lanes used are very quiet
and are not through roads so
there is almost no traffic.

Refreshments: At the Visitors
Centre. The Bull PH on the far
side of the lake about half way
round the circuit, at Three Leg
Cross.

Cycle Hire: Open at weekends
May, June and September.
Open daily July and August.

Scotney Castle. *AA Picture Library*

ALONG THE NORTH DOWNS WAY
(West from Charing towards Maidstone)

Unlike the South Downs Way, which has
bridlepath status along its whole length
and can therefore be cycled in its entirety,
the North Downs Way alternates between
footpath (where you are NOT allowed to
cycle) and bridleway or byway (where
you may). This ride uses a short section of
the trail (also known as the Pilgrims Way)
to the west of Charing. You may well wish
to combine this ride with a visit to Leeds
Castle, just a mile south of the end of the
route at Hollingbourne.
NB. At times this route uses tracks along
field edges and should not be attempted
after prolonged rain or in the winter.
It is not suitable for lightweight bikes.

Background and Places of Interest

● **The North Downs Way**
This follows the chalk range which runs from
the White Cliffs of Dover to the Hogs Back near
Guildford. Used by pilgrims in distant times as
they made their pilgrimage to Canterbury.

● **Leeds Castle**
(East of Maidstone, south of Hollingbourne)
One of the most romantic and oldest castles in
England. In the 9th century, this was the site of
a manor of the Saxon royal family. Listed in the
Domesday Book, this castle has been a Norman
stronghold, a royal residence to six of England's
medieval queens, a playground and palace
to Henry VIII and a private home. Attractions
include the Culpeper Garden, Wood Garden
and Pavilion Garden, the aviary and the maze
and grotto. Tel: 01622 765400.

● **Pluckley**
(6 miles southwest of Charing)
Said to be the most haunted village in England.
The ghosts are now joined by the more cheerful
Ma and Pop Larkin from the televison comedy
series The Darling Buds of May, which was
filmed here.

Starting Point: Charing, on the A20 between
Maidstone and Ashford.

Parking: Car park in Charing, follow signs.

Distance: 8.5 miles (17 miles round trip).

Maps: Ordnance Survey Landranger
Sheets 188 and 189.

Hills: A short steep hill at the start to get from
the car park on to the North Downs Way. There
is a drop of 200ft down into Hollingbourne, thus
a climb of the same distance on the return
trip. In general the ride is gently undulating.

Surface: Variable. From tarmac at best to a
track along a field edge at worst.

ROUTE 29
North Downs Way

Leeds Castle. *AA Picture Library* Inset: *Nick Cotton*

Roads and road crossings: The A252, a busy road, must be crossed north of Charing. There are three stretches of quiet lanes, two of less than 0.5 mile and one of about 1.5 miles.

Refreshments: Lots of choice in Charing. The Dirty Habit PH in Hollingbourne.

Route Instructions: 1. Go uphill past the Kings Head PH through the village of Charing. WITH EXTREME CARE cross the busy A252 on to the track opposite and shortly turn left at the T-junction of tracks on to the North Downs Way/Pilgrims Way.

2. At the first road, turn right then left. The following stretch may get muddy in the winter and may be bumpy in summer (the going gets easier towards Hollingbourne).

3. At the second road, go straight ahead, then shortly, at the third road, bear left downhill for 300yds, then on a sharp left-hand bend, turn right on to a track.

4. Continue in the same direction for a further 5.5 miles on a mixture of lanes and tracks following signs for the North Downs Way/Pilgrims Way as far as the Dirty Habit PH in Hollingbourne. It is worth turning left at the pub for 200yds to see the magnificent Elizabethan manor house (or with the use of the OS Sheet 188 you may wish to cycle on to Leeds Castle).

THE ROYAL MILITARY CANAL

(West from Hythe on the Saxon Shore Way)

Unlike the neighbouring counties of East and
West Sussex, there are no dismantled railways
which have been developed as cycle trails in
Kent, and aside from the rough circuit around
Bewl Water, no specific provision for easy,
traffic-free cycling. There is some Forestry
Commission land open to cycling (see page 106).
A recent study by Sustrans has put forward a
series of proposals for vehicle-free routes
through Kent, including a section of the
Millennium Route, a cycle-friendly route which
will run 1,000 miles from Dover to Inverness and
will be in place by the year 2000. This is merely
part of the 6,500-mile National Cycle Network
which is due to be completed by the year 2005.
The ride described here (together with the North
Downs ride) uses sections of bridleway that are
in good enough condition to ride in summer. The
route runs alongside the Royal Military Canal
which was built in 1804 as a defence against
Napoleon.

Background and Places of Interest

• Hythe

This ancient Cinque Port was very prosperous in the
12th and 13th centuries. Now it is a popular seaside
resort. It is a terminus of the Romney, Hythe and
Dymchurch narrow gauge railway. You can travel
across the 'Smugglers Country' of Romney Marsh
behind a ⅓ full-size steam locomotive. There are cafes
and gift shops at all main stations and a Toy and Model
Museum at New Romney.

• Port Lympne Zoo Park

Historic mansion in 300 acres. Rhinos, elephants, lions.
Safari trailer in season. Cafes, gift shops and picnic
areas. Tel: 01303 264646.

• The White Cliffs Experience

(Market Square, Dover)
Voted England's 'Visitor Attraction of the Year' in 1991.
Step back over 2,000 years and witness the Roman
invasion of Britain. Pick your way through the embers
of a 1940s Dover street following an air raid.
Open seven days a week. Tel: 01304 214566.

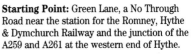

Starting Point: Green Lane, a No Through Road near the station for the Romney, Hythe & Dymchurch Railway and the junction of the A259 and A261 at the western end of Hythe.

Parking: On either of the parallel roads which lead into or out of the western end of Hythe, near the railway station.

Distance: 2.5 miles on good track (5 miles round trip). You can continue further west, but the track becomes very narrow through the woods.

Map: Ordnance Survey Landranger Sheet 189.

Hills: None.

Surface: Good gravel or firm earth track as far as the wood. It becomes rougher once into the wood.

Roads and road crossings: Getting to the start requires some care. After that, no danger.

Refreshments: Lots of choice in Hythe. Pub at Botolph's Bridge (turn left at first road crossing).

Route Instructions:

1. From the junction of the A259 and the A261, by the traffic lights at the western end of Hythe, cross the bridge over the A261 (heading north towards Ashford) then turn first left immediately after the bridge on to Green Lane, a No Through Road.

2. You can either follow the grassy track alongside the canal or the parallel, slightly lower gravel track to your right. Continue as far as the wood when the track becomes narrow and winds its way between the trees.

3. It is suggested that you turn around at this point, but there is nothing to stop you continuing in the same direction for some distance.

Romney, Hythe and Dymchurch Railway

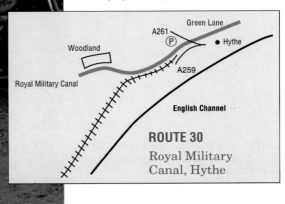

ROUTE 30
Royal Military Canal, Hythe

Listed below are some other places in the Southeast of England where it is possible to cycle away from traffic without too much difficulty, either in Essex Country Parks or along one of the three long-distance trails (the North Downs Way, the South Downs Way and the Ridgeway) that run through the region.

ESSEX

There are possibilities for cycling in several of the Country Parks in Essex along the trails marked for horses. The quality varies and they are best avoided after rain. The parks are as follows :

Belhus Woods (Jct 30/M25)	(73 hectares) (01708) 865628
Cudmore Grove (South of Colchester)	(43 hectares) (01206) 383868
Hadleigh Castle (East of Basildon)	(185 hectares) (01702) 551072
Hainault Forest (Northwest of Romford)	(119 hectares) 0181 - 500 7353
Langdon Hills (South of Basildon)	(136 hectares) (01269) 542066
Thorndon (South of Brentwood)	(151 hectares) (01277) 211250
Weald (West of Brentwood)	(195 hectares) (01277) 261343

THE RIDGEWAY/ ICKNIELD WAY

A long distance trail open to cyclists from West Kennett (near Avebury) to Princes Risborough. A 10-mile stretch is described in Route 5. The longest rideable section runs west from the Thames at Streatley up on to the Berkshire Downs, across the Lambourn Downs and past Swindon to near Marlborough, a distance of 35 miles. The route is well signposted and immense improvements have been made in the last few years to repair the deep ruts caused by the four-wheel-drive vehicles which have a right to use the track. Mountain bikes are recommended if you intend to do the whole route.

THE NORTH DOWNS WAY

The North Downs Way is an official long-distance footpath which means that it is much better signposted and maintained than any ordinary right of way and therefore easier to follow. However, its status alternates between footpath, bridleway and byway and you are NOT allowed to cycle on it where it is a footpath. A 7-mile byway section east of Maidstone is described in Route 29. There is a long stretch between Dorking and Guildford which has bridleway status, but apart from these two sections, you will have to look carefully at an Ordnance Survey map to see whether you are allowed to cycle along the North Downs Way.

THE SOUTH DOWNS WAY

By contrast with the North Downs Way, the South Downs Way is a bridleway along its entire length and would make a good challenge to a fit cyclist on a good mountain bike. It runs for 105 miles west from Winchester to Eastbourne. Three short sections along the South Downs Way are described in Routes 23, 24 and 25 where you start at the top of the ridge and explore the trail for a short distance either side of the starting point, maintaining height and enjoying magnificent views both out to sea

Facing Picture: Jack and Jill Windmills, Clayton. *AA Picture Library*

The theory is that there are 2,000 miles of towpaths in England and Wales, offering flat, vehicle-free cycling. The reality is that only a fraction of the towpath network is suitable for cycling: the rest is too narrow, overgrown, muddy and rough. There is obviously much room for improvement, and certain Waterways Boards, in conjunction with local authorities and the Countryside Commission, have made immense progress in improving towpaths for all user groups.

The Southeast of the country is well served, with long stretches of good-quality towpaths alongside all the waterways which radiate out from London. However, even the areas which have a reasonable surface are often busy with anglers and walkers, so cycle slowly, use your bell and give way to other towpath users. (Follow the Waterways Code for Cyclists, right.)

Three of the best exits from London are along canal towpaths:

1. The Grand Union starting from near Paddington (Route 6).

2. Regent's Canal/the Lee Navigation from the eastern end of the Islington Tunnel (Route 11).

3. The Basingstoke Canal which links with the Thames at Weybridge via a section of the Wey Navigation (Routes 15 and 16).

For the rest of the canal network please refer to the map and to the addresses and phone numbers of the local Waterways Board covering your area. There is no overall guideline about cycling on towpaths: some authorities issue a permit and charge for it, others issue a free permit; some have opened up the whole towpath to cyclists, others only allow cycling on certain sections. The most up to date information can be obtained from your local Waterways Board.

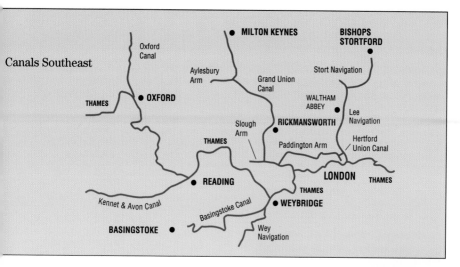

Canals Southeast

MILTON KEYNES

BISHOPS STORTFORD

Oxford Canal

Aylesbury Arm

Stort Navigation

Grand Union Canal

THAMES

OXFORD

WALTHAM ABBEY

Lee Navigation

Slough Arm

RICKMANSWORTH

THAMES

Hertford Union Canal

Paddington Arm

LONDON

THAMES

READING

THAMES

Kennet & Avon Canal

WEYBRIDGE

Basingstoke Canal

BASINGSTOKE

Wey Navigation

The addresses and phone numbers are as follows:

• Oxford and Grand Union Canal North

British Waterways, The Stop House, Braunston, Northamptonshire NN11 7JQ (Tel: 01788 890666).

• Grand Union Canal South

British Waterways, Marsworth Junction, Watery Lane, Marsworth, Tring, Hertfordshire HP23 4LZ (Tel: 01442 825938).

• London, Lee and Stort Waterways

British Waterways, The Toll House, Delamere Terrace, Little Venice, London W2 6ND (Tel: 0171 286 6101).

• Kennet and Avon Canal

British Waterways, Bath Road, Devizes, Wiltshire SN10 1HB (Tel: 01380 722859).

• Basingstoke Canal

Basingstoke Canal Authority, Ash Lock Depot, Government Road, Aldershot, Hampshire GU11 2PS (Tel: 01252 370073). River Wey and Godalming Navigation Office, National Trust, Dapdune Wharf, Wharf Road, Guildford, Surrey GU1 4RR (Tel: 01483 561389).

The Waterways Code for Cyclists

1. Access paths can be steep and slippery — join the towing path with care.
2. Always give way to other people on the towing path and warn them of your approach. A 'hello' and 'thank you' mean a lot. Be prepared to dismount if the path is busy with pedestrians or anglers.

Canal towpaths are flat and make for extremely pleasant cycling. *Nick Cotton*

3. You must dismount and push your cycle if the path narrows, or passes through a low bridge or alongside a lock.
4. Ride at a gentle pace, in a single file and do not bunch.
5. Never race — you have water on one side of you.
6. Watch out when passing moored boats — there may be mooring spikes concealed on the path
7. Take particular care on wet or uneven surfaces, and don't worsen them by skidding.
8. Never cycle along towing paths in the dark.
9. Towing paths are not generally suitable for organised cycling events, but the local Waterways Manager may give permission.
10. If you encounter a dangerous hazard, please notify the Waterways Manager at the regional office.

Please remember you are responsible for your own and others' safety! You are only allowed to cycle the towing paths if you follow this code.

The Forestry Commission owns many thousands of acres of land in the area covered by this book and has, by and large, adopted an enlightened approach to cycling in its woodlands. The broad rule of thumb is that you are allowed to ride on the hard, stone-based forestry roads which provide excellent opportunities for safe, family cycling. You are NOT allowed to cycle in the woodland away from these hard tracks and should pay attention to any signs which may indicate a temporary or permanent restriction on cycling (normally on walkers' trails or where forestry operations are in progress).

In some places, the forest authorities have even waymarked a trail for cyclists. However, open access is not universally the case, and in some woodlands you are only allowed on tracks where there is a statutory right of way, namely bridleways and byways.

This may all sound a little confusing, but the Forestry Commission is extremely helpful and normally has good reasons for restricting access. The forests are working environments where heavy machinery is often being used to fell or plant trees and whenever work is in progress there will be restrictions on recreational use.

A phone call or a letter to your local Forest Enterprise office should clarify the situation (addresses and phone numbers listed below). In order to simplify matters as much as possible, forestry areas have been divided into two categories:

(A) sites where a trail has been waymarked for cyclists

(B) sites where there is an open access policy (except for walkers' trails).

The best maps to use for exploring Forestry Commission woodland are the most up-to-date Ordnance Survey Pathfinder maps, scale 1:25,000, which tend to be reasonably accurate. Some woodlands are covered by leaflets produced by the Forest Enterprise offices, which are listed below.

PLEASE NOTE. It must be stressed that there are many different user-groups enjoying the woodlands, so courtesy and consideration should be shown at all times to walkers and horse riders. The fact that a bike can travel faster than a pedestrian does not give you any priority; indeed priority normally lies with the walker or the horse rider. Use a bell to give warning of your presence and say thank you to people who step aside for you.

A. FORESTRY WITH WAYMARKED TRAILS

FC1. Aston Hill Woods, 3 miles northeast of Wendover. Follow the A4011 Wendover/Tring road out of Wendover for 2.5 miles then turn right on a minor road towards St Leonards and Buckland Common. There is a car park on the left after 0.5 mile. The whole woods are open to mountain bikers. Much of it is fairly steep. A leaflet is available from: Chilterns Forest District Office, Upper Icknield Way, Aston Clinton, Aylesbury, Bucks HP22 5NF (0296 625825)

NB. There is NO cycling in the adjoining Wendover Woods.

FC2. Alice Holt Forest. Lies 2.5 miles south of Wrecclesham just off the A325 Farnham to Petersfield road at Bucks Horn Oak and is well

Stockfile

signposted. A 4-mile waymarked family trail. Visitor Centre and Forest Shop.

FC3. West Walk, North Boarhunt. 4 miles north of Fareham on the A32, take the B2177 out of Wickham towards North Boarhunt then first left for a mile to get to the car park at the start of the waymarked mountain bike trail. The trail is about 2 miles long.

FC4. Queen Elizabeth Country Park, just off the A3 three miles south of Petersfield. There are several waymarked trails in the park. A leaflet is available at the Visitor Centre, which is open at the weekends in the winter and seven days a week from spring to autumn.

FC5. Houghton Forest, 3 miles north of Arundel, just off the roundabout at the junction of the A29 and A284. A 5.5-mile route for mountain bikes.

Details of all the above the routes can be obtained from: Forest Enterprise, Downs & Chilterns Forest District, Bucks Horn Oak, Farnham, Surrey GU10 4LS. Tel: 01420 23666.

FC6 & 7 Friston Forest, 4 miles west of Eastbourne on the A259. A 5-mile family trail and a tough, technical 7-mile mountain bike trail.

FC8 Bedgebury Forest, north of Hawkhurst, Kent. Turn left off the A229 2 miles north of Hawkhurst. Waymarked 5-mile family trail.

B. FORESTRY WITH AN OPEN ACCESS POLICY ON THE HARD FORESTRY ROADS

You will need to use an Ordnance Survey map in conjunction with the bare-bone details below to locate the woodlands. As stated above, if you really want to explore the hard roads on Forestry Commission land then the most up-to-date Ordnance Survey 1:25,000 map is the most practical. Once you have arrived at the woodland (there is no guarantee that you will always find a car park) signs will indicate the boundaries of the Forestry Commission holdings and inform you about any restrictions in place as a result of planting or felling operations.

• Oxfordshire, Buckinghamshire, Berkshire

Aston Hill Woods/Wendover Woods (see section (A) above).

• Bedfordshire

1. Maulden Wood, 8 miles south of Bedford, between the A6 and Maulden.

2. Rowney Warren Wood, 9 miles southeast of Bedford on the A600 (north of Chicksands).

For further information write to Forest Enterprise, Northants Forest District, Top Lodge, Fineshade, Corby, Northants NN17 3BB. Tel: 01780 444394.

• Hampshire, Surrey, West Sussex

4. Bramshill Plantation, Warren Heath, Eversley Common and Yately Heath Wood. Either side of the A30 to the west of Camberley.

5. Crowthorne Wood between Bracknell and Camberley.

6. Black Wood and Micheldever Wood, 8 miles southwest of Basingstoke, either side of the A33.

7. Chawton Park Wood and Bushy Leaze Wood to the southwest of Alton.

8. West Wood, Parnholt Wood and Ampfield Wood west and southwest of Winchester.

9. Botley Wood and West Walk between Southampton and Portsmouth.

10. Woodland to the south of Petersfield, from the Queen Elizabeth Country Park east to West Harting Down and Uppark.

11. Woodland to the southeast of Midhurst. East from the A286 at Cocking to the A285.

12. Chiseldown and Eartham Wood, either side of the A285 south of Petworth.

13. Houghton Forest and Rewell Wood northwest of Arundel.

14. Woodland in the triangle formed by Chiddingfold, Plaistow and Dunsfold to the east of Haslemere.

15. Netley Heath, Ranmore Common, Abinger Forest, west of Dorking, either side of the A25 road to Guildford.

Details (but no leaflets) about the above areas can be obtained from: Forest Enterprise, Downs and Chilterns Forest District, Bucks Horn Oak, Farnham, Surrey GU10 4LS (Tel: 01420 23666).

• Kent and East Sussex

16. Wilmington Wood, Abbots Wood, Nates Wood, north of Eastbourne.

17. Friston Forest, west of Eastbourne.

18. Bedgebury Forest, northwest of Hawkhurst

19. Hemsted Forest, to the east of Cranbrook.

20. King's Wood, north of Ashford and east of Challock.

21. Denge Wood, southwest of Canterbury and southeast of Chilham.

22. Covert Wood, Elhampark Wood, Park Wood and West Wood to the south of Canterbury and the southwest of Barham.

23. Clowes Wood, north of Canterbury.

Details (but no leaflets) about the above areas can be obtained from: Forest Enterprise, Weald District, Goudhurst, Cranbrook, Kent TN17 2SL. (Tel: 01580 211044).

Stockfile

A very useful publication with details of cycling leaflets covering the whole country is called Cycle A-way! costs £4.00 and is available from: Cyclists' Touring Club, Cotterell House, 69, Meadrow, Godalming, Surrey GU7 3HS Tel: 01483 417217.

BEDFORDSHIRE

One fold-out leaflet with eight rides of between 10 and 33 miles. Send SAE and 40p to: DEED, Administration and Property, Bedfordshire County Council, County Hall, Bedford MK42 9AP. Tel: 01234 228799.

BERKSHIRE

1. *Round Berkshire Cycle Route* Large, free fold-out leaflet with details of the 140-mile waymarked county route. Available from Babtie Group, Berkshire County Council, Shire Hall, Shinfield Park, Reading RG2 9XG.
Tel: 0118 923 4561.
2. *On Your Bike — a Guide to Cycle Routes in and around Reading* Large, free fold-out leaflet with details of Reading's cycle facilities. available from Babtie Group (see above).

BUCKINGHAMSHIRE

1. *Milton Keynes Redway Guide* Comprehensive map of the cycle network in Milton Keynes. Costs £1.00 from Milton Keynes Tourist Information Centre, The Food Centre, 411 Secklow Gate East, Central Milton Keynes MK9 3NE. Tel: 01908 232525.
2. *Three Rides in Milton Keynes* Leaflet with details of three rides of between 6 and 24 miles in the Milton Keynes area (20p). Available from same address as above.
3. Other leaflets from: Environmental Services Dept, Buckinghamshire County Council, County Offices, Aylesbury HP20 1UY.

CAMBRIDGESHIRE

Three packs of leaflets, each costing £1.50
1. Five rounds around the Cambridge Green Belt area of 12-26 miles.
2. Ten rides in the Fens and around Ely, March and Wisbech of 11-25 miles.
3. Twelve rides in the Ouse Valley around Huntingdon, St Ives and St Neots of 5-24 miles. Available from: Access and Recreation Dept, Cambridgeshire County Council, Shire Hall, Cambridgeshire CB3 0AP. Tel: 01223 718403.

ESSEX

Essex County Council has produced an impressive array of leaflets and booklets about cycling in the county. Most are free, some are not. Cheques should be made payable to 'Essex County Council'. All the leaflets described below are available from: Essex Tourism, Essex County Planning Dept, County Hall, Chelmsford, Essex CM1 1LF. Tel: 01245 437081/437548.

A. OFFROAD

1. *Flitch Way* Free leaflet with details of the whole of the Flitch Way from west of Takely to Braintree. (The eastern section, from Little Dunmow to Braintree, is described in Route 4, page 28.)
2. *Blackwater Rail Trail* Witham-Maldon railway path (free)
3. *Bridleways of Brentwood* three leaflets (free).
4. *Enjoy Cycling in Lee Valley Park* A route from Waltham Abbey to Broxbourne (free).
5. *Summer Country Rides* six mountain bike rides in Essex (£2.50).

B. ON ROAD

1. *The Essex Cycle Route* An excellent booklet (£1.00) with details of a 250-mile road ride through the county, including information about cycle shops and accommodation along the way.
2. *Ongar, Matching and the Lavers* A 17-mile ride from Ongar Leisure Centre (free).
3. Cycle Tours around Braintree District (free)
4. *Uttlesford: A Cyclist Guide* Routes around Dunmow/Thaxted (free).
5. *Dedham to Bures Circular Cycle Route* (30p).
6. *Colchester Cycling Campaign Leisure Cycling Routes* Pack of seven leaflets describing road rides of between 12 and 40 miles, starting from Colchester (£1.50).

C. URBAN

1. *Cycle Routes in Harlow* (25p).
2. *Cycle Routes in Chelmsford* (25p).
3. *Cycling in Colchester* (25p).
4. *Witham Cycle Ways* Maldon Road to Chipping Hill (free).

HAMPSHIRE

1. *Offroad Cycle Trails* (pack one) Pack of 12 laminated leaflets with rides of between 6 and 26 miles.

2. *Offroad Cycle Trails* (pack two) Second pack of 12 laminated leaflets with more rides of between 2.5 and 23 miles.
Each pack costs £3.50 and is available by sending a cheque payable to 'Hampshire County Council' to Information Centre, Hampshire County Council, Mottisfont Court, High Street, Winchester, Hants SO23 8ZB. Tel: 01962 846002.
3. *Discover East Hampshire by Bike* Laminated, colour leaflet describing a 22-mile road route starting from Petersfield. Available (free) from the above address.

HERTFORDSHIRE

1. *Cycling in the Hertfordshire Countryside* Pack of nine leaflets describing 10 road rides of between 13 and 27 miles. Available (free) from: Environment Dept, Hertfordshire County Council, County Hall, Hertford, Herts SG13 8DN. Tel: 01992 555257.

KENT

1. *The Weald on Wheels* Free leaflet describing a 32-mile road route between Tenterden and Tunbridge Wells. Available from Planning Dept, Kent County Council, Springfield House, Maidstone, Kent ME14 2LX. Tel: 01622 671411.
2. *Cathedral to Coast* Signed cycle routes between Canterbury, Folkestone and Dover Leaflet with map of the 50-mile route. Costs £1.00, payable to Kent County Council and available from address above.
3. *Parish Pedals* Four laminated leaflets with details of routes in the Weald of Kent. Costs £1.00, payable to Kent County Council and available from address above.

OXFORDSHIRE

1. *The Oxfordshire Cycleway* A guide including 12 route sheets describing the 200-mile county cycle ride on minor roads. Also includes details of six circular route options of rides between 29 and 178 miles. Available by sending £3.70 (inc p+p), payable to Oxfordshire County Council to Countryside Service, Dept Leisure and Arts, Oxfordshire County Council, Holton, Oxford OX33 1QQ. Tel: 01865 810266.

2. *Discover Oxfordshire by Bike* A pack of nine leaflets detailing offroad circular rides in the Chilterns and around Charlbury. Cost: £1.50, see above for details of where to send money.

SURREY

1. *Surrey Cycleway* Large fold-out leaflet describing the waymarked 86-mile route around the lanes of Surrey. Available from County Cycling Officer, Surrey County Council, County Hall, Kingston KT1 2DT. Tel: 0181 541 8044.
2. *Action Packs* Pack of 11 leaflets with details of offroad routes in Surrey. Send £4.40 to Action Packs, The Booking Hall, Boxhill Station, West Humble St, West Humble RH5 6BT. Tel: 01306 886944.
3. *Norbury Park Family Offroad Cycle Route* Leaflet describing 2.5-mile route in Norbury Park, northwest of Dorking. Tel: 01372 386881.
4. *Pathways to Health at Horton Country Park* Leaflet with map of the cycle trail in Horton Country Park (northwest of Epsom). Tel: 01372 741191.
5. *Common Sense Cycling on Epsom Common* Leaflet describing the 3-mile offroad trail on Epsom Common. Available from The Community Services Dept, Epsom and Ewell Borough Council, Town Hall, The Parade, Epsom, Surrey KT1 5BY. Tel: 01372 732466.

SUSSEX

1. *Cycling East Sussex* Leaflet with details of guided rides of varying degrees of difficulty, time and distance. Available from East Sussex County Council, Transport & Environment, Sackville House, Lewes BN7 1YA. Tel: 01273 481654.
2. *Cycling in West Sussex* A general information leaflet about cycling in the county. Available from County Planning Officer, West Sussex County Council, County Hall, Tower Street, Chichester PO19 1RL. Tel: 01243 777610.
3. *Town to Down Shoreham* Free leaflet with map showing the paths and bridleways linking the coastal towns with the downs. Available from West Sussex address above.

Local authorities are the obvious organisations to contact to find out what cycle routes exist locally, what plans there are for the future and for reporting any complaints you may have about the provision of cycle routes in your area. Their addresses are as follows:

BEDFORDSHIRE
DEED, Administration and Property, DEED, County Hall, Bedford MK42 9AP. Tel: 01234 228488.

BERKSHIRE
Babtie Group, Shire Hall, Shinfield Park, Reading RG2 9XG. Tel: 0118 923 4561.

BUCKINGHAMSHIRE
Environmental Services Dept, County Offices, Aylesbury HP20 1UY. Tel: 01296 383158.

CAMBRIDGESHIRE
Environment Division, Environment and Transport, Castle Court, Shire Hall, Cambridgeshire CB3 0AP. Tel: 01223 718403

ESSEX
Planning Dept, County Hall, Chelmsford, Essex CM1 1LF. Tel: 01245 437081/437548.

HAMPSHIRE
Recreation and Heritage Dept, Mottisfont Court, High Street, Winchester, Hants SO23 8ZF. Tel: 01962 846002.

HERTFORDSHIRE
Environment Dept, County Hall, Hertford, Herts SG13 8DN. Tel: 01992 555257.

KENT
Planning Dept, Springfield House, Maidstone, Kent ME14 2LL. Tel: 01622 671411.

OXFORDSHIRE
Countryside Service, Dept Leisure & Arts, Holton, Oxford OX33 1QQ. Tel: 01865 810266.

SURREY
County Cycling Officer, County Hall, Kingston KT1 2DT. Tel: 0181 541 8044.

EAST SUSSEX
Transport & Environment Dept, Sackville House, Lewes BN7 1YA. Tel: 01273 481654/482257.

WEST SUSSEX
Planning Dept, County Hall, Tower Street, Chichester PO19 1RL. Tel: 01243 777610.

For addresses of British Waterway Boards and Forestry Commission regional offices, please see the appropriate chapters.

THE CYCLISTS TOURING CLUB (CTC)
Cotterell House, 69 Meadrow, Godalming, Surrey GU7 3HS (Tel: 01483 417217).
This is Britain's largest cycling organisation, promoting recreational and utility cycling. The CTC provides touring and technical advice, legal aid and insurance, and campaigns to improve facilities and opportunities for all cyclists.

THE CYCLE CAMPAIGN NETWORK
National liaison organisation, bringing together information about Britain's many local cycle campaigns. For details of your local campaign group send SAE to CCN, 54-57 Allison Street, Digbeth, Birmingham B5 5TH.

SUSTRANS
35 King Street, Bristol BS1 4DZ (Tel: 0117 926 8893).
Sustrans won £42million of lottery funds to help build the 6,500-mile National Cycle Network which will be completed by the year 2005. The Millennium Routes, covering the first 2,500 miles of the network, will be ready by the year 2000, including a route stretching from Dover to Inverness. The network will use a mixture of quiet lanes, forestry tracks, canal towpaths, dismantled railways and purpose-built cycleways.

BIKE 1
Freepost (Gl 2064), Fleet, Hampshire GU13 8B. Tel: 01252 624022.

BIKE EVENTS
Tel: 01225 480130.
Organises 15 major charity rides from May to October, including the London to Cambridge and Manchester to Blackpool rides.

OPEN AIR
Tel: 0117 922 7768.
Organises one-day charity rides throughout the year, including the annual To the Lighthouse and London to Windsor events.